G

070.5
ONE...
$15.95

One Hundred and Fifty Years
of Publishing

————

1837-1987

34 Beacon Street

One Hundred and Fifty Years
of Publishing 9526

1837–1987

LITTLE, BROWN AND COMPANY
BOSTON   TORONTO

FIRST EDITION

Library of Congress Cataloging-in-Publication Data

One hundred and fifty years of publishing,
1837–1987.

Bibliography: p.
Includes index.
1. Little, Brown and Company—History.
2. Publishers and publishing—Massachusetts—
Boston—History.   I. Little, Brown and Company.
II. Title: 150 years of publishing, 1837–1987.
Z473.L7632053   1987   070.5'0974461   86-27679
ISBN 0-316-52791-2

—

Published simultaneously in Canada
by Little, Brown & Company (Canada) Limited

PRINTED IN THE UNITED STATES OF AMERICA

Contents

List of Illustrations

Illustration credits appear on page 222

Publisher's Note

One Hundred and Fifty Years of Publishing, 1837–1987 is an informal account of Little, Brown and Company from its beginning to the present. As such, it records the highlights of 150 years of publishing books and materials in the United States.

Every reasonable effort has been taken to include significant events and relevant contributions. Nevertheless, the text does not cite hundreds of staff members whose dedication and diligence made it possible for the company to survive many crises and challenges and prosper over so many decades. Publishing is a people business and depends on staff, most of all on the authors and artists whose talent is reflected in the works they write and create. Alas, as in the case of staff, it has not been possible to record all the thousands of good titles published over such a long span.

It should also be said that the narrative focuses on the strengths and successes of our activities. Needless to say, there were many disappointments, for personnel and

coveted books were lost to other houses; expected sales
didn't materialize; and external factors such as economic
recession and political conflict also played a part. In any
case, book publishing is a very unpredictable enterprise,
and one can be thankful for and appreciative of consoli-
dated success over a long period.

In 1937 and 1962, Little, Brown published its centennial and one hundred twenty-fifth histories, which were
prepared by the staff and written by an anonymous
author who was also a staff member. Now, however,
it seems appropriate to depart from this tradition and
recognize the individual who wrote the first draft and
conducted and supervised the research for this sesquicentennial history. The person is Fred Belliveau, who
spent well over a year in this assignment after he left the
Medical Division and before his retirement. Fred was assisted in his research by Paul Twist, a free-lance special-
ist, and the text was refined by the expert wordsmiths
Perdita Burlingame and Betsy Pitha, both Little, Brown
editorial veterans. The book was designed by Robert
Lowe and the jacket by Pearl Lau. For these efforts we
are deeply grateful.

One Hundred and Fifty Years
of Publishing

1837–1987

1

"A Copartnership"

O n June 29, 1837, these three small advertisements
appeared in the *Boston Daily Advertiser:*

NOTICE.—The copartnership heretofore existing between
the subscribers, under the firm of HILLIARD, GRAY & CO.
is hereby dissolved by mutual consent. H. GRAY and CHARLES
BROWN are authorized to adjust the concerns of said firm.
                                    HARRISON GRAY,
                                    JAMES BROWN,
                                    CHARLES BROWN.
    Boston, June 22, 1837.   Je 29

COPARTNERSHIP.— The undersigned will continue the
Publishing and Bookselling business, under the firm of
HILLIARD, GRAY & CO. at the new building, Water street,
corner of Devonshire.   HARRISON GRAY,
                                    CHARLES BROWN.
    Boston, June 22, 1837.   Je 29

COPARTNERSHIP NOTICE. — The undersigned have
formed a copartnership, under the firm of CHARLES C.
LITTLE & CO., for the purpose of Publishing, Importing and
Selling Books, and have taken the old stand of Hilliard, Gray &
Co., No. 112, Washington street, and purchased their Law, For-
eign and Miscellaneous stock.
                                    CHARLES C. LITTLE,
        Je 29   istf   JAMES BROWN.

The "copartnership" in the third item signals the beginning of one of America's most venerable publishing
houses, one of the few antedating the Civil War that survive today.

The venture undertaken by Charles C. Little and
James Brown commenced in a world of change and
challenge, innovation and growth. Oliver Wendell
Holmes, Nathaniel Hawthorne, Henry Wadsworth
Longfellow, and Ralph Waldo Emerson were all con-
tributing to the flowering of New England. William Ellery Channing, William Lloyd Garrison, and Wendell
Phillips were urging social reform. To the west, Chicago
was incorporated as a city and Texas recognized as a nation. In Great Britain, the youthful Victoria assumed the
throne, beginning an era that would last more than sixty
years. Louis Philippe maintained a precarious hold on
the shaky French throne. In Italy and Ireland, move-
ments for national independence and unity were stirring,
and the antipodean city of Melbourne, Australia, was
duly christened.

Following the inauguration of Martin Van Buren, a financial panic had ensued in America, leading to suspen-
sion of specie payment, a large federal deficit, and high
interest rates. Yet there were those who felt that the
country was on the verge of enormous growth. Steam
railroads were beginning to revitalize transportation and
many other businesses, and entrepreneurs were convinced that the area west of the Mississippi would soon
open up — an expectation realized only twelve years
later, when the California gold rush began. Many predicted, and Charles Little and James Brown must have
sensed, that a great period of economic prosperity was at
hand.

Brown and Little were also, no doubt, aware of the developing technology in book publishing. Lithography
had been introduced in 1819, and cheaper methods of

bookbinding in 1827. Old wooden printing presses had been replaced with iron ones, and Boston's first cylinder press began operation in 1829. The typecasting machine, an invention of even greater importance, was to come into being in 1838, and stereotypy, commercialized in England in 1800, was about to become established in the United States. Mechanical typesetting, which alleviated the labor costs of hand-set type, and stereotypy, which permitted many copies to be made from metal cast from a papier-mâché mold of the type, speeded up the processes of setting type and of printing.

Moreover, the demand for books in the new and growing republic was high. There was an ever-expanding market for history, law, and what we today would call textbooks. It was, in short, a good year for the founding of a new publishing house.

Of course, like any family, corporation, or nation, Little, Brown had predecessors. The firm's origins date to 1784, when Ebenezer Battelle opened a bookstore in Boston on what was then Marlborough Street. Over the next twenty-eight years, the store changed hands four times, acquiring in the process a name, a circulating library, and a small publishing program. In 1812, the Boston Bookstore, as it was then called, was acquired by Jacob Cummings. Thereupon Cummings entered into a partnership with William Hilliard, proprietor of the University Bookstore in Cambridge.

Hilliard, an intellectual, ambitious, and farsighted man, saw Harvard students as the perfect market for the books the new partnership was producing. In Cummings, a schoolteacher and author of many of the books the firm now published, Hilliard found the ideal partner.

Cummings's *Ancient and Modern School Geography*, which sold at 75 cents a copy with an additional 87¼ cents for the companion atlas, was required reading for admission to Harvard. In fact, most of the books on the Cummings, Hilliard list were required reading at the college.

Having gained a firm foothold with the Harvard students, Cummings and Hilliard took the next step — signing up Harvard professors as their authors. Some of the early Harvard publications were *"Lectures on Rhetoric and Oratory* by John Quincy Adams, Late Professor of Rhetoric and Oratory in Harvard College"[1] and *"Elements of Logic* by Levi Hedge, Professor of Logic, Metaphysicks and Ethicks." Cummings and Hilliard did not, however, confine themselves to the Harvard marketplace. Their books were sold throughout New England, and they imported unusual and scholarly volumes from all parts of Europe.

In 1815, their business expanding, Cummings and Hilliard hired an apprentice, Timothy Harrington Carter. Starting at the age of sixteen with such duties as the printing of maps, the folding and stitching of pamphlets, and the manufacture of inks, Carter soon revealed uncommon abilities. During his five-year apprenticeship he expanded the business greatly, and after he sold some twenty thousand dollars' worth of books on a trip to Baltimore, it became apparent that he was an excellent salesman.

After Cummings's death Carter was admitted to the partnership, and beginning in 1823 the firm was known as Carter, Hilliard & Company. Carter not only persuaded Hilliard to undertake the publication of law books, so that for the first time various "Digests of Cases and Common Laws" began to appear under the firm's imprint, but also was instrumental in helping Hilliard make his largest and most important sale.

Carter had hired his brother Richard to open up new markets for the firm, especially in Virginia. There Richard Carter met Joseph Coolidge, a fellow Bostonian who was married to Thomas Jefferson's granddaughter and who, as a Harvard graduate, was knowledgeable about the Boston bookselling firm. Coolidge and Carter urged Jefferson to employ Carter, Hilliard as supplier to the library of the new University of Virginia, pointing out Hilliard's exceptional ability to secure books from the many European markets. With great success Hilliard carried out this task from 1824 to 1826: "It was an outstanding enterprise by which a Boston bookseller helped not merely to build the library of a great University, but, in that building, to extend one step further the intellectual frontiers of the East. He had helped develop Harvard. Now he could help establish the University of Virginia."[2]

Throughout the 1820s the firm expanded rapidly, and additional associates and employees came and went, including a new partner, Harrison Gray, who added his name to the firm's in 1827. Carter left the firm that year and in 1829 started the Old Corner Bookstore with his brother, but not before he had hired a young clerk named Charles C. Little in 1821, to help with the growing list of law books. Meanwhile, the University Bookstore in Cambridge was prospering, and in 1818 Professor Levi Hedge had recommended to Hilliard that he hire James Brown as a clerk. By 1826 Brown was a partner in the Cambridge bookstore, with an interest in the Boston shop, and in 1827 Little became a partner in Hilliard, Gray & Company. Since the two firms were so closely affiliated, by the end of the decade Brown and Little had become very good friends.

When William Hilliard died in 1836, the dynamic Little was left with two weak partners — Gray and John H. Wilkins, who had been made a partner in 1827. Thereupon he and Brown decided to form their own partnership and take over the Hilliard, Gray shop, along with the firm's law, foreign, and miscellaneous stock and the continuing projects in law and history. What was left of Hilliard, Gray — mostly schoolbooks — moved to a shop at the corner of Water and Devonshire streets, where it maintained a modest existence until 1843.

Thus the appearance of the three advertisements in the June 1837 issue of the *Advertiser*. Over the years since 1784 and the establishment of Battelle's bookstore to the founding of Little, Brown, there had been many changes, but there was a continuing tradition established by the talented William Hilliard, a tradition best described by the word "quality." Now Little and Brown, friends, equal partners, hard workers, were prepared to carry on that tradition and to shape the future of the firm through their own personalities.

Described as "energetic, sagacious, upright and prudent," Charles Little was the descendant of a pioneer, George Little, who came to Newbury, Massachusetts, in 1640. Charles was born in Kennebunk, Maine, on July 25, 1799, and like many young men of his time decided to leave the farm and head for the city. In Boston he got a job with a shipping company on Long Wharf and later spent a winter in Charleston, South Carolina. Shipping, however, was not to his taste, and upon his return to

Boston he was hired as a clerk by Timothy Carter in 1821. His interest in and emphasis on legal publishing remained with him throughout his long and distinguished publishing career.

Little's rapid and steady success was due in large measure to his business acumen. After he and Brown formed their partnership, it was Little who developed much of the early publishing list. The epitome of the self-made nineteenth-century businessman, he had a strong civic and entrepreneurial sense. He served twice as a Cambridge selectman and for two years was a member of the lower house of the Massachusetts legislature. Little also owned a great deal of real estate in Cambridge and was one of a group who formed the Cambridge Gas Light Company in 1852, introduced a water system from Fresh Pond in 1856, and started a horse railroad from Harvard Square to Bowdoin Square in Boston. Little also served as president of the Charles River National Bank.

In the true tradition of the virtuous apprentice, Charles Little married the boss's daughter. By Sarah Anne Hilliard he had four sons and a daughter. After Sarah Anne's death he married the daughter of Henry Wheaton, a well-known writer on international law.

About James Brown we know more, thanks to a memoir written by critic and essayist George S. Hillard. Brown's was a different personality from that of his partner: "One senses in the lack of more positive information, that he [Brown] was a foil for the conservative Little."[3] Brown was one of those men whom everyone liked. All the traditional superlatives could be offered about him; all the traditional virtues applied. He, too, epitomized the nineteenth-century success story — a poor boy making good by dint of hard work, talent, and intelligence.

Charles C. Little

James Brown

Brown was born in Acton, Massachusetts, on May 19,
1800. His father, Joseph, one of the first to volunteer for
service in the colonial army, was wounded at Bunker
Hill. After the war he settled on a farm in Acton. James
Brown's mother, Abigail Putnam, had a fairly good
eduation and had worked as a teacher before her mar-
riage. Since James's health as a child was somewhat precarious, his mother shielded him from the rigors of farm
life and allowed him to spend his time with her closetfuls
of books.

After Joseph Brown's death in 1813, Abigail did not
have enough money to keep the family together, so the
thirteen-year-old James moved to a nearby farm. Two
years later he decided to look for a job in Cambridge,
yearning for the intellectual life available in that city. He
could not have been more fortunate, for he became a
servant in the home of Professor Levi Hedge. There he
was surrounded by gentility, intelligence, and kindness,
and when Hedge discovered that Brown was bright and
scholarly, he tutored the boy privately in mathematics
and Latin and permitted him to browse at will in the
splendid Hedge library. The four years Brown spent with
the Hedge family were a time of intellectual blossoming
for the young man, and it was Hedge, as we know, who
arranged for Brown's apprenticeship with William Hilliard.

Thereafter, Brown was steadily successful. He was well
suited to his occupation, and his occupation was well
suited for him. In his memoir George Hillard says:

> He was born with the feelings and instincts of a gentle-
> man. He had an unerring power of observation and a
> delicate tact that never failed him. His manners were

winning because they were the natural language of a good heart and a sweet temper; and their effect was increased by the open and ingenuous expression of his countenance. But his success in this department came mainly from those sources from which the whole success of his life was derived — from his entire truthfulness and perfect honesty. . . . Everyone who dealt with Mr. Brown felt that he was dealing with a perfectly honest man, and that every word that fell from him could be taken at its full value, with no qualifications and reservations.[4]

Brown married Mary Anne Perry in May 1825, and for some years they lived in Cambridge, but in 1840 his love of nature led him to move his family to a comfortable country house in Watertown. Brown was a kind and loving father, and his five children grew up in an affectionate and happy household. Mary Anne died in 1844, and in 1846 Brown married Mary Derby Hobbs of Waltham.

In their business relationship, Brown and Little each concentrated on the things they did best, neither interfering with the other. Little managed the law list and Brown the importation and sale of foreign books. Together they made a formidable team.

2

The New Firm Prospers

When Little and Brown formed their partnership
in 1837 and took over the assets of Hilliard,
Gray, they inherited a good many uncompleted publishing projects. These included a series of American biographies, the works of Benjamin Franklin, and the writings
of George Washington, all edited by historian Jared
Sparks. The new firm acquired as well its predecessor's
quarters at 112 Washington Street, in the heart of Boston's Publishers' Row. The number was later changed to
254, and the four-story building, known as the College
Building because it belonged to Harvard College, was
replaced in 1860 by a five-story granite-faced structure,
which Little, Brown then occupied in its entirety.

The imprint used by the house in these years varied;
on title pages it was Charles C. Little and James Brown,
or occasionally C. C. Little and J. Brown. In 1847 the
name of the firm was officially changed to Little, Brown
and Company, and thus it has remained.

Although a respectable publishing program was developing, the heart of the business lay in bookselling and importing. The walls of the tall, high-beamed building on Washington Street were lined with long shelves filled with the red-labeled, sheepskin-bound sets of Massachusetts Supreme Judicial Court reports and other legal works. On opposite walls were displayed choice volumes of English literature, finely bound in polished calf or half-levant — books well suited for a gentleman's library. Some of these books came from private libraries that the firm had bought for resale. In the *Christian Register and Boston Observer* of October 28, 1837, Little, Brown announced that it had more than six thousand volumes of classic works for sale, most of them from England, including the Johnson and Stevens edition of Shakespeare in fifteen volumes and Scott's works of Dryden in eighteen. There were also upwards of three hundred volumes of sermons by the best-known English theologians, copies of the *North American Review,* and the complete collections of the Massachusetts Historical Society, all for sale "at very low prices."

In charge of the retail side of the business was newcomer Augustus Flagg, who joined the firm in 1838 and stayed for forty-six years. Flagg's background was similar to those of Little and Brown. Born on a farm in Worcester, Massachusetts, on January 17, 1818, he began his career with a Worcester bookseller and came to Boston in search of a job in 1838. Finding no openings there, he took a position in New York but was delighted when scarcely two weeks later a clerkship at Little, Brown was offered him. Flagg's keen eye and sound judgment for which books would sell and in what quantities rapidly led to his wide acquaintance with book dealers. He was admitted to partnership in the firm in 1846, and he, Charles Little, and James Brown made up an extremely effective triumvirate.

In the 1840s Washington Street was the center of Boston publishing and bookselling. On the floors above Little, Brown in the Washington Street building was the firm of Phillips & Sampson, booksellers and publishers of law, classical, and school books. Opposite, at the corner of Washington and School streets, was the famous Old Corner Bookstore, once managed by Richard and Timothy Carter, after 1846 run by George D. Ticknor and Company and as of 1854 by publishers Ticknor and Fields. A few doors to the south, T.O.H. Perry Burnham had an antiquarian bookstore, and two buildings away E. P. Dutton held sway for many years before moving to New York. At least six other notable houses were nearby, many of them specializing in religious books, the chief genre of Boston publishing at the time.

What has been called one of the pleasantest chapters in the history of American publishing was written during these years. All of Boston's literary, religious, and legal notables passed through the doors dotting Publishers' Row. The Little, Brown store became a haunt for members of the bar, legal writers, and Harvard literati. For a number of years an informal club met in James Brown's office at noon to talk over literary matters and discuss the merits of new publications. The shop was a favorite browsing place for Daniel Webster, an unflagging buyer of books. Augustus Flagg once remarked, "His manners were generally very quiet, but sometimes he would get warmed up, and then look for thunder!" Edward Everett relished the foreign imports, while George Bancroft purchased everything he could in the field of American his-

tory. Lawyer Rufus Choate was irresistibly attracted by
the shelves of classical works. One day he spied a number
that he wanted but could not afford. Reported Flagg:
"Finally he could stand it no longer and said, 'I want
those books and I will take them under one condition;
that I shall not be dunned for them under three thousand years.' He was always as simple as a child. He
would ask about books in a most charming manner,
though he knew a great deal more about them than
booksellers did."[1]

The imported English books that filled up so much of
the store were the result of James Brown's labors. Brown
knew the book trade better than most of his contemporaries. He and Little insisted on well-made, attractive
books, becoming known for creating a market in
America for the finest editions of English works. At the
same time the partners were canny enough to realize that
the public taste would be more likely to improve if the
best and most beautiful books could be obtained at reasonable prices. Brown believed that many books of quality could be introduced to the American public if British
publishers could be persuaded to sell as few as five hundred copies of a title at little over the cost for printing
and paper. So successfully did he preach this gospel that
notable works of poetry, biography, and history were frequently sold in the United States for much lower prices
than they commanded in England.

In 1841 Brown took the first of five trips to the Continent and to England, where he met the leading booksellers and publishers. His way had been paved by the
historian William Prescott, who wrote to Richard Bent-
ley, his London publisher, on May 30, 1841: "This letter
will be handed to you by Mr. Brown, one of the publish-

ers of my history and a principal publisher in the United States. He visits Europe to make some arrangements connected with his business, and any facilities or information that you can give him in this way will be a favor to me."[2]

The British were greatly impressed by Brown's knowledge, charm, and affability. The English publisher John Murray became so close a friend that Brown named his youngest son after him. Brown bought the best new and standard English books, and his efforts were met with approval and even excitement in Boston, where eager collectors awaited the newly arrived shipments from London, Paris, Brussels, and Le Havre.

Brown's choices were the classic works that educated people would buy and read: the works of John Milton, Francis Bacon, and Edmund Spenser; the plays of Shakespeare; the poetry of Coleridge; the speeches and writings of Edmund Burke and William Pitt; Adam Smith's *Wealth of Nations;* Daniel Defoe's *Robinson Crusoe.* For a mere $1.25 one could purchase a volume in the series called the Library of Entertaining Knowledge, which dealt with almost everything, from insect architecture and the people of New Zealand to the Elgin Marbles and a history of British costume.

Nor was the Continent neglected. The *Fables* of La Fontaine, the works of Rabelais, the plays of Molière (in both French and English) were available, along with books in Latin, Spanish, and Italian. There were books on architecture, engineering, painting, religion, travel. Some things in publishing never change: Among Brown's acquisitions was a work entitled *New Theory of the Influence of Variety in Diet in Health and Disease.*

Augustus Flagg

Little, Brown and Company's first home
at 112 Washington Street

3

Building the Law Book List

Whyhen Timothy Carter hired Charles Little in
1821, the law list of Cummings, Hilliard was already burgeoning. By 1837, under Charles C. Little &
Company, it was well established and highly successful.
Charles Little's special talent in the field of law publishing would make the Little, Brown law list one of the
greatest in the United States.

In their first catalogue, Little and Brown stated: "We
shall continue to make the sale of law books our principal business," and it was primarily from efforts in this
area that the company quickly got onto a sound financial footing. The catalogue shows that the new company
had nine hundred law titles for sale, most of them imports from England. At that time the ties to the English
legal system were still strong, and English law books
had considerable appeal. Such works as Sir William
Blackstone's *Commentaries on the Laws of England* and Sir
Edward Coke's *Institutes,* which formed the very founda-
tions of English law, were listed in Little, Brown's catalogue.

Nevertheless, the new firm did not rely exclusively on British imports. The publishing of original works by American jurists rapidly became an intrinsic part of Little, Brown's program. Three notable writers who brought great luster to Little, Brown over the years were Joseph Story, one of the founders of equity jurisprudence in the United States; Chancellor James Kent, whose monumental work on the common law has had enormous impact on our judicial system; and Simon Greenleaf, whose work on evidence is a cornerstone of American law. From the earliest times, writers on the law have held a central place in the history of thought; men such as Story, Kent, and Greenleaf were not merely lawyers but scholars of broad knowledge whose works transcended their time.

Joseph Story was born in Marblehead, Massachusetts, in 1779 and graduated from Harvard College in 1798. As was customary then, he learned the law through apprenticeship with other lawyers. His remarkable talent was soon recognized, and he was appointed an associate justice of the Supreme Court by President James Madison in 1811. Eighteen years later, Story also became the first Dane Professor of Law at Harvard and was instrumental in establishing the Harvard Law School.

It was his Harvard emolument that enabled Story to pay for the publication of his famous *Commentaries*. During much of the nineteenth century, authors did not enjoy the contractual arrangements that are now the norm, whereby a publisher produces a book and sells it at his own expense, paying a royalty on the sales to the writer. It was common then for authors such as Story to pay for the making of stereotypes of their books, which then became their personal property and were leased to the publisher for a number of years, as determined by contract. Occasionally authors also paid for their own printing.

Story developed his Harvard lectures into nine volumes, all of which had national significance, some of which became important abroad. The first four *Commentaries* were published by Hilliard, Gray; the fifth appeared under the Little, Brown imprint. The 1837 catalogue lists the titles inherited from Hilliard, Gray: *Bailments* (1832), *On the Constitution of the United States* (three volumes, 1833), *Conflicts of Law* (1834), and *Equity Jurisprudence* (two volumes, 1836). The subsequent Little, Brown titles were *Equity Pleadings* (1838), *Agency* (1839), *Partnership* (1841), *Bills of Exchange* (1843), and *Promissory Notes* (1845).

That one man, with few American cases as precedents, could prepare these large, technical volumes in a period of thirteen years seems incredible — particularly when one remembers that Story was simultaneously a Supreme Court justice and a Harvard professor. Even by nineteenth-century standards, it must have been very taxing, but the results justified Story's labors. The *Commentaries* met with widespread and immediate success and had a profound effect on the development of the American legal system. They were also profitable, earning for the author a reported ten thousand dollars a year.

In person, Story was a vigorous, active, restless man, and above all a great conversationalist. Augustus Flagg often saw Story at Little, Brown's bookstore, where he was a frequent caller:

He would come in and lay out large supplies of old books, principally works on civil law, volume after volume, and in all languages. He was always full of humor, and was so much of a talker that it has hard for anyone to get in a word. One time Chancellor Kent came into the store. . . . Story and Kent had not met for a long time. Kent was also a tremendous talker, and it was amusing to watch the race of words between them. When Story would get the floor he would stick to it as long as possible, then Kent would get ahead, struggling with equal vigor to hold on. They seemed so delighted to see one another, when they met, it was difficult for either one to find an opportunity to speak.[1]

James Kent was one of the those unusual men whose claim to fame came late in life — in his case, after his retirement. Born near Brewster, New York, in 1763, he followed his grandfather and father to Yale. After graduation he read law, then embarked on a distinguished political and legal career in New York State that included his appointment as the first professor of law at Columbia University and culminated in his being made chancellor of the New York Court of Chancery, then the highest judicial office in the state. To this position Kent brought a mind expertly trained in the principles of the common law, and his thorough study of English legal theory and practice helped him place the American system of equity on a firm foundation.

When, at the age of sixty, Kent was forced to retire from the bench, he embarked upon one of the most productive periods in his life, for his son, also a judge, suggested that his father turn his legal lectures into a book. Thus Kent began the monumental task of putting together in one reference work the common law of the young nation.

The four volumes of Kent's *Commentaries on American Law* appeared between 1826 and 1830 under the imprint of first Cummings, Hilliard and then Hilliard, Gray. Unlike Story, Kent would not allow his work to be stereotyped, since he insisted on making changes in the book right up to printing time. He had the volumes set into type and printed at his own expense, afterward turning them over to his publisher to sell. The cost of producing the first volumes was $1,076.27, a considerable sum for Kent, who was not a man of means. Had this first volume not been a commercial success, Kent probably would not have continued, but luckily its importance was immediately recognized, and sales exceeded the author's highest expectations.

With this encouragement, Kent devoted himself full-time to the *Commentaries*. The second volume appeared in December 1827, the third in October 1828, and the fourth in April 1830. "Your work," wrote Joseph Story in 1836, "must forever remain the true standard for all future American text writers." In 1837 Charles Sumner commented, "When I think of the good you have done, in promoting the study of jurisprudence by the publication of your Commentaries . . . I cannot but envy you the feelings which you must enjoy. The mighty tribute of gratitude is silently offered to you from every student of the law in our whole country."[2]

Kent had charted new ground and filled a great need. His masterpiece was so accurate, well reasoned, clear, and simple that it quickly made its way into the hands of all legal practitioners. "The whole country, from ocean to ocean, was permeated by the same principles, the same deductions, and practically the same laws based, for the most part, upon the life work of New York's greatest lawyer."[3] The success of the *Commentaries* led to many editions published by Little, Brown and edited by many eminent men, including Justice Oliver Wendell Holmes.

Simon Greenleaf, the third seminal legal writer, was born in 1783 in Newburyport, Massachusetts, and moved to Maine as a child. There he studied law and joined a practice near Portland. During his first twelve years of practice he had time to read widely on the common law, and when he moved to Portland in 1818, his reputation quickly propelled him into a top position in the local judiciary. In 1820 he was appointed reporter of the Maine Supreme Judicial Court, where his reports were highly valued for their accuracy and clarity.

In 1833 Joseph Story offered Greenleaf the Royall Professorship of Law at Harvard. When Story died, twelve years later, the younger man succeeded to the Dane Professorship and became head of the Harvard Law School. Largely through the efforts of these two men, Harvard began its rise to the eminent position it holds today. Story and Greenleaf complemented each other almost perfectly — the former was quick, brilliant, enthusiastic, the latter deliberate, thorough. In the words of the *Law Reporter,* "Story prepared the soil and Greenleaf sowed the seed."[4]

Greenleaf in 1842 published with Little, Brown his *Treatise on the Law of Evidence.* It was instantly hailed as the best work on the subject, and Greenleaf went on to

Simon Greenleaf

Joseph Story

James Kent

publish the second volume in 1846 and the third in 1853. *Evidence* became *the* American authority and had many successive editions, the sixteenth of which was prepared by John Henry Wigmore, who himself subsequently produced his own monumental work on evidence, published by Little, Brown in 1904.

These three great ninteenth-century writers saved the common law for the United States by summing up English law of the seventeenth and eighteenth centuries and placing it in a new context for the new nation. Their achievement is the foundation of our legal system today, and the publication of their works made Little, Brown's place in the annals of legal publishing secure.

4

Building
the History Book List

Even as respected legal writers began to devote their attention to the law of the steadily maturing nation, so an equally renowned group of historians focused on its past. Three — Jared Sparks, George Bancroft, and Francis Parkman — addressed the story of young America; William Prescott chose to tell about the Spanish conquests in the New World. All were Bostonians, and all were published by Little, Brown.

Prescott, born in 1796, the victim during his Harvard days of a cruel accident that maimed his left eye, was wealthy enough to hire researchers, readers, and copiers for assistance in preparing his manuscripts. Even so, writing was very difficult for him. Prescott nevertheless made a remarkable literary and scholarly contribution to American history.

Having completed the manuscript of the *History of the Reign of Ferdinand and Isabella, the Catholic* in 1837, Prescott consulted his friends in the Boston–Cambridge intellectual community, including Sparks and Bancroft. They convinced him to have the book stereotyped by the well-known firm of Folsom, Wells, and Thurston. In April, Prescott went to the American Stationers' Company to arrange for publication of the work; a few months later the company went bankrupt, forced out of business by the panic of 1837. Prescott then turned to Little, Brown and on May 14, 1838, signed a contract with the firm for *Ferdinand and Isabella.*

> It was [Little and Brown's] business-world vigor that attracted Prescott to them, and the contract of 1838 was formulated solely as a business arrangement. As successive impressions of his book emerged bearing the Little, Brown & Company imprint, Prescott routinely endorsed the contract as he accepted note after note, obligations which seemingly were paid with such regularity that no strain occurred between author and publisher.[1]

The contract stipulated that Little, Brown was to be allowed a five-year period in which to print and publish a minimum of 1,700 copies of *Ferdinand and Isabella* from Prescott's stereotype plates. None of the printings would be for fewer than 250 copies, and the author's high standards for paper, printing, and binding were written into the agreement. Little, Brown's exclusive rights were to last until November 1, 1843. Prescott was to be paid at the rate of $1.75 per copy every six months in the form of promissory notes and was to retain the European and abridgement rights for the work. Thus for this period Prescott received $2,975; later printings and an abridgement brought him even more.

The three volumes of *Ferdinand and Isabella,* which sold for $7.50 retail, were bound in tan cloth with a floriated design to which the cream-colored endpapers and the gold-stamped spines lent a note of added richness. The books were printed on fine-quality paper with wide margins, double-columned footnotes, and maps where appropriate. Each volume had a frontispiece: Isabella in Volume I, Ferdinand in Volume II, and Cardinal Ximenes de Cisneros in the third volume. To Jared Sparks, Prescott wrote: "I think you will admit that Queen Isabella herself would have been gratified to have seen herself exhibited in so beautiful a dress."[2]

Ferdinand and Isabella was widely praised. The *North American Review* (Jared Sparks's journal) called it "a large and valuable historical work, such as rarely appears, being the fruit of long labor and learned research." The *Washington Globe* wrote, "Mr. Prescott has done honor, not only to himself, but to his country." And the British *Edinburgh Review* commented, "Mr. Prescott's work is one of the most successful historical productions of our time." Prescott, whose advertising acumen modern authors might envy, wasted no time in using such reviews as promotion "puffs" for the book.

Prescott was a businessman as well as a historian. When his five-year contract with Little, Brown expired, he decided to transfer subsequent publication of the volumes to Harper and Brothers, who offered him more substantial earnings, and then to the Boston publisher Phillips & Sampson, which offered still greater sums. Still, there was no ill will when Prescott left Little, Brown. The firm continued to feature his books in the store, and Prescott did not hesitate to drop off chapters of his next manuscript, *The Conquest of Mexico,* at Little, Brown for its perusal, although the book was under contract with Harper. The modern reader may make what he will of this story; the facts remain that Prescott was "relentless in his efforts to promote his books" and thus moved from publisher to publisher, but also that Little, Brown did its best by him and was proud to publish his *Ferdinand and Isabella* and promote his later volumes.[3]

Jared Sparks, the historian to whom Prescott had turned for advice, was a quite different sort of author. Born in Wilmington, Connecticut, in 1789, Sparks was a child prodigy. Given only a modest education, he started teaching at the age of eighteen, but friends were so impressed by his brilliance that they sent him to Phillips Exeter Academy in New Hampshire, where he spent two years. After a Harvard education, he became managing editor of the *North American Review* in 1815. In 1823 Sparks bought the *Review* from Edward Everett and built it up into the most influential literary and scholarly periodical in the United States.

Charles Folsom, scholar, printer, and producer of the stereotypes for Prescott's *Ferdinand and Isabella,* gave Sparks the idea of preparing a collection of the writings of George Washington in 1827. Although there was some difficulty in obtaining the cooperation of Judge Bushrod Washington, George Washington's nephew and owner of his letters, eventually a promise of income from the project did the trick, and Sparks embarked upon the labor that would last for the next ten years.

Not all of Sparks's time and energy were spent on either the Washington project or the *North American Review.* During the years 1827 to 1840 he produced a prodigious amount of historical writing. Several volumes

about the Revolutionary era were contracted with Hilliard, Gray and were eventually inherited by Little,
Brown. In 1834, still deep in the Washington project,
Sparks undertook to edit the works of Benjamin Franklin. Ten volumes were published between 1836 and 1840,
the first volume being a life of Franklin and the rest consisting of his letters and other papers. *The Works of Benjamin Franklin* is considered Sparks's best work apart from
his Washington volumes. Though he was not a lively
writer like his colleague George Bancroft, he had a clear
narrative style and an appreciation of the nation's his-
toric documents that was communicated to his readers.

During this same period, Sparks was also involved in a
major publishing project, first with Hilliard, Gray and
then with Little, Brown. This was the editing of the Library of American Biography series, short lives of important Americans narrated by a variety of authors. The
series had been planned in 1832, at which time Sparks
had so many irons in the fire that he tried to persuade
Bancroft to take over the project. Bancroft declined, and
Hilliard, Gray insisted that Sparks remain as editor. The
first part of the series appeared between 1834 and 1838
and consisted of ten volumes; the second part (1844–
1847) had fifteen. (A series bearing the same title has
been issued by Little, Brown since 1954.)

Sparks was clearly a man of many parts and unlimited
energy. As if he did not have enough to occupy his time,
in 1838 he was offered the McLean Professorship of History at Harvard — the first professorship of history at
any American university — and in 1849 he became the
president of Harvard. He died in 1866 (one hopes after a
few years of well-earned rest), leaving one of those

records of prodigious achievement that seem to distinguish so many of his nineteenth-century colleagues and a reputation for kindling new interest in American history and the men who made it.[4]

Like Prescott, Sparks often consulted his fellow historian George Bancroft. Bancroft has been called the father of American history because of his ten-volume work, *A History of the United States*, published from 1834 to 1874, revised and cut to six volumes in 1876, and completely revised again and published from 1883 to 1885, when Bancroft was in his eighties. Bancroft — one of the major authors Little, Brown inherited from Hilliard, Gray — made a typical arrangement with his publishers: The books were manufactured at the author's expense and then turned over to the publisher for distribution. Writing to Little, Brown in 1869, Bancroft said, "I had invested much capital in the work.... The expenses of various kinds in collecting materials, mss. and books, in journeys, time employed in researches, writing, copyists, money paid for examination, etc., etc., might be put without exaggeration at fifty or even seventy-five thousand dollars."[5]

The first scholar to plan a comprehensive study of the nation's past, Bancroft was also the first American historian to recognize the importance of the colonial period, foreign relations, and the frontier as forces in U.S. history. Influenced by the German "scientific" school of history (he had been educated at the University of Göttingen), intensely patriotic, a Jacksonian Democrat who freed American history from its dependence on Federalist myths, Bancroft approached his study with the

conviction that in America was to be found the highest
form of government.

Extravagant praise was lavished on the *History* and its
author as the several volumes appeared. Edward Everett
wrote to Bancroft, "I think you have written a Work
which will last while the memory of America lasts"; and
later, "I take great pleasure in reflecting that I predicted
at the outset the brilliant success that is crowning your
life-labor." William Prescott remarked, "His colonial
history establishes his title to a place among the great
historical writers of the age," while Washington Irving
wrote in 1852, "Your work rises as it progresses, gaining
in unity of subject and in moral grandeur as it approaches the great national theme." Still another note of
approval came from Ralph Waldo Emerson: "The history is richer not only in anecdotes of great men but of
the great heart of towns and provinces than I dared believe; and — what surprised and charmed me — it starts
tears and almost makes them overflow on many and
many a page. . . . It is a noble matter, and I am heartily
glad to have it nobly treated."[6]

Bancroft did not devote the forty years between the
publication of the first and last volumes of his *History* entirely to its writing. He was appointed secretary of the
navy in 1845, during which time he established Annapolis as the U.S. Naval Academy; in the same period he was
acting secretary of war, issuing the orders that sent General Zachary Taylor into Mexico. In 1846 he was appointed minister to Great Britain, and in 1867 minister
to Berlin. Still, his years abroad provided him with the
opportunity to collect more data for the remaining volumes of the *History,* so obviously it was never far from his

William Prescott

Jared Sparks

George Bancroft

Francis Parkman

mind. In 1910, almost twenty years after his death, he was elected to the Hall of Fame, and the *History* was named "the most popular American historical work of the nineteenth century."

Perhaps it was the fame of Bancroft and Sparks that drew a younger man, Francis Parkman, to Little, Brown. A student of Sparks's at Harvard, Parkman by the age of eighteen had already decided on the themes of what were to be his historical writings. Parkman was born in 1823 into a Boston family of wealth and social standing, and suffered throughout his adult life from a disorder of the nervous system that frequently incapacitated him. Like Prescott, he too had great difficulty with his sight, but he did not let his infirmities stand in his way. Little, Brown was to publish Parkman's books for more than forty years, futher securing its position as publisher of the best American historical writing.

In his youth Parkman had traveled to the West, living for a time with the Sioux Indians and gathering material for his first book, *The California and Oregon Trail,* published in 1849. His next volume, *The History of the Conspiracy of Pontiac,* came out only two and half years later, a remarkable feat when one considers that his physical problems had become acute and permitted him to write only a few lines a day. Much of his research material (most of it in French) had to be obtained from the libraries of Europe and needed to be read to him because of his failing vision.

His next project absorbed him for the rest of his life. This was the seven-part series called France and England in North America, which covered the period from the beginning of French colonization in America until the British conquest of New France in 1763. Parkman originally skipped over the first forty-eight years of the eighteenth century because he feared he might not live long enough to complete the entire series, and he was determined to cover the French and Indian War campaigns of Generals Wolfe and Montcalm. Thus *Montcalm and Wolfe* appeared in 1884, and the seventh volume, *A Half-Century of Conflict,* in 1892, a year before Parkman's death. In this final book he examined the period between 1700 and 1748, thus rounding out the series.

The work was reviewed in the United States, Canada, and England as "a masterpiece of military history and the first authentic, full, sustained and worthy narrative of these momentous events and extraordinary men." "The completion of this history," said the *New York Times,* "is an event that should awaken interest wherever historical genius can be appreciated. . . . [Parkman's] work ranks with the most brilliant and lasting historical undertakings that have marked the past fifty years." James Russell Lowell observed in the *Century Illustrated Monthly Magazine,* "Mr. Parkman's familiarity with the scenery of his narratives is so intimate, his memory of the eye is so vivid, as almost to persuade us that we ourselves have seen what he describes"; the *Nation* said, "Mr. Parkman's painstaking research has earned him a place in the front rank of American writers of history."[7] Parkman remains notable not only for his voluminous and accurate research but also for his vigorous and beautiful writing style.

There were, of course, other works of history published by Little, Brown during the middle decades of the nineteenth century, but Prescott, Sparks, Bancroft, and Parkman were probably the firm's most significant authors, making an indelible mark in the annals of historical writing, picking themes that were "waiting" to be covered. Little, Brown made its mark in publishing them. The study of American history came of age with the scholarly achievements of these illustrious men.

5

Courtesy of the Trade

The 1840s and 1850s in the United States were marked by change, confusion, and divisiveness as the country grew. Settlement west of the Mississippi, exploration of California and the discovery of gold there, and acquisition of land from Mexico following the Mexican War enormously expanded the territory of the United States; inevitably, there arose the question of whether these were to be slave states or free. The Compromise of 1850 and the founding of the Republican party only exacerbated the tension. Moreover, such rapid expansion, coupled with equally swift developments in technology and transportation, produced an economic climate that was anything but stable.

At the same time, these changes were having a profound effect upon the publishing industry. Expansion of the country's land meant expansion of the country's population, and consequently more readers. Growth of the railroads led to greater availability of published material. Changes in the postal laws and something so basic as the invention of adhesive postage stamps made mailings to prospective customers much less costly.

Amidst all these changes, Little, Brown resolutely pursued its course, following its stated policy "to sell and publish standard works of a high grade — books of a grave, solid and substantial character."[1] Little, Brown steadfastly adhered to James Brown's emphasis on imports and Charles Little's on legal publications, and made its ventures into the field of history, as we have seen. One writer has commented about this period: "Boston publishers were moribund with tradition . . . and provincialism. . . . Little, Brown was satisfied with its profits on law books and its conservative publishing policy."[2] Conservative it may have been, yet the policy enabled Little, Brown to survive the panics of 1857 and, later, 1873. By comparison, other publishers were ready to take chances. Ticknor and Fields, established in Boston in 1854 by James T. Fields and William D. Ticknor, was willing to publish the works of such men as Hawthorne, John Greenleaf Whittier, and Henry David Thoreau.

Another competitor in Boston publishing was soon to appear. In 1848 Henry Houghton bought into the printing company of Freeman and Bolles, whose principal customer was Little, Brown. When Bolles and with him Houghton moved into a building in Cambridge owned by Little, Brown, the relationship became very close. James Brown was fond of Henry Houghton, and Houghton looked up to Brown as "the most far-sighted and courageous publisher he had known, a man who saw his business in a large way and yet had the resolution and decision to keep clear of speculative ventures."[3] For

Whig Mass Meeting on Boston Common, September 19, 1844.
The house at 34 Beacon Street, which Little, Brown
acquired in 1909, appears to the left of the flag.

some years the major printing of Little, Brown's books continued at Houghton's expanding firm, known as the Riverside Press, but in March 1855 James Brown died, apparently of diabetic complications, and Houghton lost his friend. Little, Brown thereafter came to feel it no longer occupied a premier position with the printer, especially when in 1863 Houghton contracted to print George and Charles Merriam's *Webster's Unabridged Dictionary.* Two days later, Little, Brown abrogated its contract on three months' notice. This sudden departure strengthened Houghton's decision to go into publishing for himself and led to the establishment of the illustrious publishing house of Houghton Mifflin.

The traditionalism that characterized Little, Brown during this period did no damage to its achievement. The catalogue of 1857 — issued twenty years after the firm began — indicates some pruning, some new ventures, and much that was the same. The law list was reduced from nine hundred titles to one hundred, and more emphasis was laid upon American rather than European authors. The enduring popularity of poetry inspired the firm in 1853 to begin a series patterned after a British one known as Pickering's Alden Poets. By 1858 the Little, Brown series included ninety-six volumes in print and thirty-one more on press, covering British poets from Chaucer to Wordsworth. Under the editorship of Francis J. Child, Boylston Professor of Rhetoric and Oratory at Harvard, these volumes were edited, designed, and printed in Boston. The small, well-produced, cloth-bound books sold extremely well.

Most of the books of English authorship in the 1857 catalogue were, however, imports and reprints — a side of the business Augustus Flagg handled after Brown's death. No fiction appeared on the list, but there were numerous works on religion, government, agriculture; anthologies of letters and essays; the dramas of Beaumont and Fletcher; Boswell's life of Johnson; and Gibbon's *Decline and Fall of the Roman Empire.* Little, Brown was also the sole distributor in the United States of the *Encyclopaedia Britannica* and the agent for Didot Frères, the Paris publisher. Like James Brown before him, Augustus Flagg made many trips to England and the Continent, looking not only for new works but also for rarities, early imprints, fine bindings, and prize editions of the classics.

Importing new books was made easy by the casual rules of the 1790 copyright law, still in force in the mid-nineteenth century. The law protected the rights of U.S. authors only in this country, so that British publishers could pirate American works; by the same token, British books were not protected here, so that American publishers could do the same. As a result, there was no standard practice for royalty payment, as we have seen. American publishers therefore found it financially advantageous to secure proofs of a British publication and put the book on the market ahead of competitors, but that was often only a temporary advantage, because a subsequent, cheaper edition, issued by another publisher, could appear and undercut the first publisher's sales.

This free-for-all was modified, however, by a developing practice called courtesy of the trade, instituted in lieu of an international copyright, and one which Little, Brown was quick to espouse. Under this policy the American publisher would pay the foreign (usually

English) counterpart an honorarium for early sheets of a book. This enabled him to start production before his rivals and ensured that those publishers who respected the policy would treat the book as if it were copyrighted by the paying publisher. As Charles Little put it, this was no more than "gentlemanly conduct, and a feeling among respectable booksellers that one ought not to interfere with the business of another."[4] After the Civil War, a refinement was added: The American house would announce its arrangement to publish an author in an advertisement in the *Commercial Advertiser,* and the date of such an announcement would constitute a claim to the book.

The treatment offered to foreign authors under the practice of courtesy of the trade varied according to the merits of the specific project. The payment of a lump sum, common until the Civil War, was largely replaced in the 1870s by the practice of offering a smaller initial payment and then a royalty on the copies sold. If the book did not recover its costs, no further payments were made. After the passage of the copyright law of 1891, such royalty payments became standard.

Gradually over these decades a more modern kind of publishing and bookselling was emerging, with centralization, an improvement of business ethics, and a national rather than a regional character. Twice a year leading auction houses in Boston, Philadelphia, and New York conducted sales of the books of all publishers. From the 1840s on, these sales, attended primarily by retail booksellers, were held exclusively in New York, and they became extremely important to publishers. In 1859, for instance, Little, Brown at one sale disposed of some twenty-five hundred volumes.

The advantage of trade sales was that they allowed a publisher to sell large amounts of stock in a short time. The disadvantage was that publishers could off-load what we today would call remaindered stock along with current books. Retail booksellers disliked the lack of price stability for current books, and small-town and country sellers would often take the remaindered books at reduced prices and not bother with new titles.

Imperfect though they were, trade sales continued throughout the 1870s, but opposition to them was growing. By 1890 they had just about passed from the scene, having been replaced by a growing corps of salesmen who packed their trunks with books, samples, and inviting brochures and were visiting booksellers across the country by the ubiquitous trains. Now, instead of the bookseller coming to the publisher, the publisher sent his emissaries to the booksellers. Two of Little, Brown's most successful future heads of house, James W. McIntyre and Arthur Thornhill, Sr., made their reputations as salesmen on the road.

6

Quotations and Quillets

Not often is a partner in a publishing house simultaneously one of its best-selling authors. Then again, not often is there a John Bartlett. Joining Little, Brown in 1863, becoming a partner in 1865 and senior partner until his retirement in 1889, Bartlett brought with him a book destined to be one of the firm's all-time classics, *Bartlett's Familiar Quotations.*

John Bartlett was born in Plymouth, Massachusetts, and at the age of sixteen, in 1836, became an apprentice bookbinder in the same University Bookstore of Cambridge that William Hilliard had owned and where James Brown got his start. A year later, "I was entered as a clerk in a bookstore," said Bartlett in a charming commentary about his career, "and found myself amid a world of books, 'in wand'ring mazes lost.' Without a guide, philosopher or friend, I plunged in, driving through the sea of books like a vessel without pilot or rudder." He continued: "My clerical duties were usually onerous, yet I always found time for study and reading; and during my active business life of fifty-two years I devoted much time to these purposes. My library was my dukedom large enough, with few exceptions, for all my wants."[1] That dukedom he later described in a small pamphlet called *A Record of Idle Hours,* which lists the books he read during his lifetime — more than five thousand. It should be noted that all of Shakespeare's works and all the novels of Sir Walter Scott each counted as just one book.

At the University Bookstore, Bartlett soon developed a reputation as an authority on practically anything written, such that the frequenters of the shop would consult him for the source of a quotation or the name of the author of a certain book. "Ask John Bartlett" became a byword, and John Bartlett usually had the answer. In 1849 he took over ownership of the store and quickly conceived the idea of publishing a collection of all those quotations his customers asked him to identify.

The idea became a reality in 1855. Bartlett published the book himself, in an edition of a thousand copies. In his brief introduction he explained his philosophy: "The object of this work is to show, to some extent, the obligations our language owes to various authors for numerous phrases and familiar quotations which have become 'household words.'" One hundred and sixty-nine authors wre represented in the book, which had 277 pages and only twenty footnotes. Quotations from the Bible and from Shakespeare made up about a third of the text; the remainder were chiefly from the British poets. A mere handful of Americans were included: Washington Irving, William Cullen Bryant, Henry Wadsworth Longfellow, James Russell Lowell. There were no quotations from Washington, Adams, or Jefferson, nor from Bartlett's contemporaries Emerson, Whitman, and Thoreau.

That they were omitted is not, in fact, surprising, for Bartlett leaned heavily on the criterion of familiarity: Quotations would not be admitted "simply on their own merits, without assurance that the general reader would readily recognize them as old friends."[2] Emerson qualified by the third edition, Whitman and Thoreau by the tenth.

Unsure of the reception of his little book, Bartlett thought an appropriate motto would be John Bunyan's quaint apology for his own work:

> Some said, "John, print it"; others said, "Not so."
> Some said, "It might do good"; others said, "No."

But the book became such an instant success that Bartlett, like Byron, awoke one morning and found himself famous.

In 1858 Bartlett sold his store and for the next four years did not engage in business. During part of the Civil War he served as volunteer paymaster in the South Atlantic Squadron. In 1863 he returned to join Little, Brown, which brought out the fourth edition of his work in that same year. For this edition, as for all of those published between 1856 and 1890, he had the help and collaboration of Rezin Augustus Wight.

Throughout his years at Little, Brown, Bartlett kept up his scholarly work, which resulted not only in the steady expansion of the *Quotations* but also in the less widely known *Shakespeare Phrase Book,* on which he and his wife worked lovingly for twenty years before its publication in 1882. A short, genial man, Bartlett also loved social life, had many close friends, and was blessed with a keen sense of humor. One of his favorite pastimes was trout and bass fishing; James Russell Lowell wrote a poem about it for him — "To Mr. John Bartlett, who had sent me a seven-pound trout." His collection of 1,014 books and 269 pamphlets about his favorite sport was presented to the Harvard College Library in 1892. Shakespearean scholar, chess expert, whist player, angler, connoisseur of letters, Bartlett died in 1905 at the age of eighty-five, as familiar a figure around Boston and Cambridge as his famous book.

Nine years after Bartlett joined Little, Brown, in 1872, disaster almost overtook the firm. Francis Parkman wrote to a friend in Paris that November:

> But the next day, Saturday, the blow fell. At seven-thirty in the evening a few stores caught fire in the most important commercial quarter of the city. The flames spread with incredible speed and fury. . . . In two or three hours the entire quarter was in flames. The spectacle was at the same time sublime and frightful. Huge solid buildings of granite or sandstone seemed to melt as if in a furnace. The whole city was threatened with destruction. . . . Little Brown & Co. fortunately escaped; the fire stopped some fifty meters from their offices and storerooms, thanks to the new post office building, which is close by. It is a vast structure of granite, brick and iron which was able to resist the flames.[3]

Little, Brown was indeed fortunate. Many publishers and allied businesses in and near the Washington Street area were virtually wiped out, and if the fire did not put an end to them, the still-vacillating national economy did a year later, in the panic of 1873. The remainder of the 1870s became a time of financial hardship and economic depression. It says much for the able leadership of Augustus Flagg, who had taken over as senior partner upon the death of Charles Little in 1869, that Little, Brown was never in difficulty.

Flagg remained senior partner until his retirement in 1884, when he was succeeded by John Bartlett, who held the position until his own retirement at the end of the decade. The other partners during this period were Thomas W. Deland, John Murray Brown (the youngest son of James Brown), and George Flagg, the brother of Augustus. Under their supervision the firm continued to publish and sell books of quality in the way it had found the best and most profitable.

Output in the field of law was varied and included much more original material than had previously been part of the Little, Brown list. Not only was there a constant flow of important works, such as *The Law of Contracts* by Theophilus Parsons and *The Common Law* by Oliver Wendell Holmes, Jr., in addition the firm was now publishing the Massachusetts statutes, the Supreme Court *Reports,* the U.S. Supreme Court *Digest,* and *Statutes at Large,* which dealt with British parliamentary law in the eighteenth century. Little, Brown also published the *American Law Review,* a quarterly sold by subscription, and, beginning in 1878, a law bulletin for lawyers announcing new books. Originally called *Quillets of the Law,* it was soon renamed, rather more prosaically, *Little, Brown and Company's Law Book Bulletin.* In keeping with the title, the *Bulletin* solemnly listed important new titles and the availability of annotated cases, but occasionally a touch of humor entered in:

"Witness, how did the quarrel begin?"
"This way, Your Honor" [witness yelling out], "You fools! You idiots!"

The Judge [interrupting]: "Do not address yourself to the jury!"

The initiation of the law bulletin inspired Little, Brown to issue in the same year a newsletter for the public, called *Books and Authors*. It spoke of the problems and expense of magazine and newspaper advertising and concluded, "This is especially the case with publishers of standard books like our own, — which appeal only to cultivated literary tastes." Indeed, the general books Little, Brown published during the seventies and eighties were, as always, intended for educated readers. The newsletter extolled the merits of *Reminiscences of Daniel Webster* by Peter Harvey (1877), a charming collection of anecdotes, history, biography, and Boswellian gossip. A poem by Shelley was printed in full. Gift-book suggestions included Plutarch's *Lives,* Izaak Walton's *Compleat Angler,* Bacon's *Essays,* and, naturally, *Bartlett's Familiar Quotations.* •

Following its own advice about not incurring mass-media advertising costs, Little, Brown brought out instead a proliferation of catalogues. One listed scientific books, "Embracing a large Collection of the best works on Architecture, Engineering, Chemistry, Metallurgy, Mathematics, Physics, Agriculture, Natural History and other Sciences." Another offered books on political economy, finance (with a separate listing of books for bankers in at least one issue), sports, games, and decorative arts. Special catalogues published each year in the pre-Christmas season touted choice illustrated works as suitable gifts, and in 1881 a catalogue of "Scarce and Interesting Books" was issued.

History, like the law, was still one of the company's

mainstays. Notable American contributions were John F. Morse's *Life of Hamilton,* John Gorham Palfrey's *History of New England,* and William Cabell Rives's *History of the Life and Times of James Madison.* From England came Thomas Babington Macaulay's *History of England* and John Stuart Mill's *Principles of Political Economy.*

British imports still figured large on the company's lists. In all its sales literature Little, Brown announced, "English books imported to order by every steamer." And in the 1870s, for the first time novels were included. Among them were Sir Walter Scott's Waverley novels and the works of William Makepeace Thackeray (in twenty volumes). Next came thirty volumes of Dickens's works and ten of Henry Fielding's. Jane Austen appeared on the list in 1875 and George Eliot a year later. Little, Brown was not the primary American publisher of these noted authors; rather, it bought rights to particular editions of their works, usually on a nonexclusive basis. At the same time John Bartlett encouraged the publication of works outside the standard British field, and such names as Victor Hugo and Honoré de Balzac appeared in Little, Brown catalogues.

Just as novels from abroad arrived in the seventies and eighties, so did children's books. Fairy tales were popular; in 1876 *German Fairy Tales* and *Grimm's Fairy-Tales* were on the list. In 1876 it was *Favorite Fairy Tales of the Mikado's Empire,* "embellished with many illustrations of most artistic design, price, 40 cents. Or on thicker paper with silk tassels, 60 cents." Fantasy was tempered by solider fare: The list of 1878 led off with Dickens's *Child's History of England* (at two dollars a copy), and the literary tastes of young readers were to be encouraged by Scott's *Lady of the Lake* and *The Lay of the Last Minstrel.*

John Bartlett

Oliver Wendell Holmes, Jr.

Thomas W. Deland

George Flagg

John Murray Brown

The importing of novels and children's books set the stage for a dramatic change in Little, Brown's publishing emphases. Learning to sell this type of book gave the firm the expertise to diversify. Hitherto there had been little reason for ventures into the risky and untested. The firm had done very well with its traditional fields of law, history, and the classics, and none of the partners was especially interested in going in any other direction. All of this changed, however, with the retirement of Augustus Flagg in 1884 and of John Bartlett in 1889. Flagg had given forty-six years of remarkable service to Little, Brown. As one Boston paper aptly put it, "The eminence of the house was due largely to his shaping and rigidly adhering to a policy which has made his firm's name a synonym for preeminent respectability and great financial strength."[4] Now the leadership was younger and interested in trying new things.

7

Best-Sellers

The decade of the 1890s marked many changes, not only for Little, Brown but for American publishing as a whole. Little, Brown's acquisition of three unusual authors — a bearded citizen of Warsaw; a small, crippled, red-haired woman; and a cantankerous admiral who feared the sea — as well as another publishing house turned it in a quite different direction from its prior concentration on law, history, and imports, and effectively made it a nationally recognized firm. At the same time, legal and technological developments profoundly altered the shape and direction of American publishing.

Probably the single most important event was the passage of the International Copyright Act of 1891. This law at last extended to foreigners copyright protection, thus superseding the casual courtesy of the trade agreements and ending the flow of cheap reprints that had flooded the country during the earlier years of the century. (Little, Brown, with its emphasis on quality imports, had never engaged in this trade.) The new law encouraged native literature by protecting American authors published abroad and stabilizing royalty payments. It also permitted more books from the Continent to be published in this country.

The best-seller arrived, in the shape of a monthly list first published by the *Bookman,* a magazine of literature and criticism, in its inaugural issue of January 1895. And the publishing industry itself changed. There were improvements in printing, typography, and design; the editorial and production functions began to be more widely separated. A movement toward standardization of trade methods and solidarity of action was taking place: maintaining of prices, training of booksellers, widening of publicity. National sales forces were formed, the members of which visited booksellers and jobbers on regular, fixed schedules. All these changes helped Little, Brown's new management to expand the firm's program and goals.

When Augustus Flagg retired in 1884, John Murray Brown became the active head of house, and in 1889, after John Bartlett's retirement, the senior partner. Perhaps even more important to the company's future was the dynamic James McIntyre, a junior partner. McIntyre, an ambitious, energetic man, had been born in Boston in 1848, and like most of his predecessors joined the firm as an apprentice, at the age of sixteen. After an initial training period, he was put in charge of the Washington Street bookstore, where he met the well-known lawyers and literati frequenting the store. Next, McIntyre went on the road, selling in New York and elsewhere. Finally, he was made editor in chief of the publishing division, the ideal position in which to mastermind the expansion into what we now call trade books. That expansion was given assurance of success because of McIntyre's encouragement of Henryk Sienkiewicz, the Polish novelist; Fannie Farmer, the small redhead; and Admiral Alfred Thayer Mahan.

Henryk Sienkiewicz was born on May 5, 1846, near Lukow in Russian Poland. Educated at the University of Warsaw, Sienkiewicz became part of a group that revolutionized Polish literature in the aftermath of the unsuccessful uprising against Russia in 1863. Sienkiewicz, noted throughout his life for his hatred of Russia, emigrated to a Polish socialist colony in California in 1876, but three years later returned to his native land to earn his living as a journalist and to begin writing a trio of historical novels that gained him an international reputation and brought him to the attention of Little, Brown.

One of Sienkiewicz's early admirers was a remarkable American linguist and translator, Jeremiah Curtin, who included Polish among the seventy-odd languages he knew. Curtin read about Sienkiewicz's first two novels, *With Fire and Sword* and *The Deluge,* in a Polish magazine and obtained copies from Poland. He found them to be of such merit that he translated them into English and arranged with his friend James McIntyre for their publication by Little, Brown. *With Fire and Sword,* published in 1890, sold 1,922 copies in its first year; *The Deluge,* published in 1891, sold 1,585 copies; and *Pan Michael,* the concluding volume of the trilogy, 2,432 copies in 1893. Although disappointed in these sales figures, Brown and McIntyre persisted in their support of Sienkiewicz and Curtin. Their perseverance paid off in 1896 with the publication of Sienkiewicz's next book, *Quo Vadis.*

Here was a real novel, unencumbered with difficult Polish names and obscure details of Polish history. This story, set in the time of Nero, was a rousing tale of Christian martyrdom and Roman debauchery, appealing to every taste. It took the country by storm, selling six hundred thousand copies within eighteen months of publication and more than a million and a half copies of the Little, Brown authorized edition by 1915. Never before had the firm published so successful a book.

To be sure, there were a few problems. Little, Brown had to share the triumph of *Quo Vadis* with other publishers because of a copyright snaggle; a pirated edition of the book put out by a Philadelphia publisher in 1897 sold in the thousands each week. Still, Little, Brown had its first big fiction best-seller and gave the author the access to Western readership that contributed to his winning the Nobel Prize for literature in 1905.

Little, Brown's next best-seller, also published in 1896, could not have been more different. This was Fannie Merritt Farmer's *Boston Cooking-School Cook Book,* which started a revolution in American cookery and eventually sold more than three million copies in various Little, Brown editions.

Servants were disappearing from the American home, and housewives were becoming more and more responsible for their own cooking. As the *Atlantic Monthly* put it:

> The original cookbook emerged at a time — not very different from our own — when women's lives were undergoing enormous changes, when fresh and dazzling possibilities clashed with traditional beliefs, and when all women felt the trembling of the earth under their feet even if they never left their kitchens. Fannie Farmer's

cookbook represented a reassuring, even stimulating way for a woman to understand her life at home. Miss Farmer believed women's responsibilities were significant ones, and she honored those tasks not with simpleminded obeisance to traditional roles, but with respect, thoughtfulness, and imagination. Her cookbook, and her career, embody a solution to social turmoil that thousands of women found compelling at the turn of the century.[1]

Throughout her career Fannie Farmer, who became known as "the mother of level measurements," stressed the scientific principles as well as the art of cooking. She used exact, uniform weights and measures instead of the older, pinch-of-this-dab-of-that scheme that had characterized handed-down recipes. The cookbook contained hundreds of recipes that she and her staff and students had tested, as well as many useful charts, tables, household hints, and menus. Its precision and firm, clear directions were just what the American public wanted.

Not that this was immediately apparent to Little, Brown, which turned down the manuscript when she first brought it in. Miss Farmer, however, was not to be deterred. She convinced McIntyre and Brown to take on three thousand copies of the book on the condition that they were printed at her own expense, and her judgment, of course, proved correct.

The eldest of four daughters, Fannie Farmer was born in Boston in 1857 and grew up in nearby Medford. In her teens she was struck probably with polio, which left her with a paralyzed left leg and a permanent limp and prevented her from attending college. When her family out of necessity began to take in boarders, Miss Farmer started to help with the cooking and soon revealed an outstanding talent. Her family then encouraged her to enter the Boston Cooking School. Her energy, intelligence, and skill made her a star pupil, and after her graduation in 1889 she was asked to join the school as assistant principal, becoming principal two years later.

In 1902, the success of her book having provided the money, Farmer established her own school, Miss Farmer's School of Cookery, and began to tour the country, lecturing and demonstrating techniques. Although she was a private person, never granting interviews or permitting Little, Brown to use her picture on book jackets, Farmer lost her shyness when she stepped onto a lecture platform. There her white dress, red hair, and bright blue eyes made her a striking figure. She also wrote with her sister a column for the *Woman's Home Companion.*

She suffered a stroke in 1908, which left both her legs paralyzed, but she continued to lecture and write until her death on January 15, 1915. The *Woman's Home Companion* could not bring itself to tell its readers of her death. Instead, for the next eleven months it ran recipes of the kind that had made Fannie Farmer and her cookbook a true American institution.

The third major book marking Little, Brown's expansion in the 1890s was Admiral Alfred Thayer Mahan's *Influence of Sea Power upon History.* "With the possible exception of Harriet Beecher Stowe's *Uncle Tom's Cabin,* published in 1852, no book written in nineteenth century America by an American had greater immediate impact on the course and direction of the nation," wrote biographer Robert Seager.[2] Mahan had a message the United

Jeremiah Curtin and Henryk Sienkiewicz

Fannie Farmer

Alfred Thayer Mahan

States wanted to hear, and he knew how to communicate it: The nation that controlled the sea, or strategic parts of it, controlled history.

Alfred Mahan was born in 1840 at West Point, where his father was professor of engineering at the U.S. Military Academy. After attending Columbia University for two years, Mahan entered the Naval Academy at Annapolis, graduating with second honors at the age of nineteen. During and after the Civil War, the future admiral commanded various ships and alternated sea duty with teaching tactics at the Newport War College — an assignment far more appropriate to his tastes and talents, for Mahan, ironically, had a thoroughgoing fear of the sea and of collision, and was nearly helpless as a practical and practicing seaman.

By October 1888 Mahan had put his War College lectures into manuscript form and started to look for a publisher. Because Scribner's had published his first book, *The Gulf and Inland Waters,* in 1883, Mahan turned to that firm first, but his manuscript was rejected on the grounds of being far too technical and specialized. For nearly a year Mahan circulated his 185,000–word manuscript among many commercial publishers, all of whom turned it down. In September 1889 a mutual friend asked James McIntyre to consider the work. McIntyre read it, saw its importance, and urged John Murray Brown to read it, too. Mahan then came to Boston, convinced Brown that it was not too technical, and *The Influence of Sea Power upon History, 1660–1783* was published in May 1890.

Not particularly original in its concepts, *Sea Power* could trace many of its ideas as far back as Xenophon, the Greek historian, who wrote in the fourth century B.C.

that control of the sea played a large part in the out-
come of land battles. The book, in addition, was difficult
reading for nonspecialists and reviewers. Nevertheless,
Mahan, a great synthesizer, was able to distill from his
many sources a clear and well-presented message: "History proved conclusively that national power, wealth,
grandeur, and security were by-products of the pos-
session and sophisticated exercise of massive sea power."[3]
In particular Mahan related this idea to the commercial
expansion of the United States, and showed how in his
opinion American national security was jeopardized by
the commercial and imperial ambitions of Europe. To
protect its own interests, said Mahan, the United States
had to expand trade outside its borders, a policy that
would require building a large maritime fleet and a navy
to protect it, to be sustained by coal and supply stations
throughout the world. These ideas, expressed in a hun-
dred-page chapter, especially appealed to the public interest.

The book was extremely well received. One of Mahan's strongest boosters was Theodore Roosevelt, who
wrote that the book was "the clearest and most instruc-
tive general work of the kind with which I am acquainted. It is a *very* good book — admirable; and I am
greatly in error if it does not become a classic." The *Critic*
of July 26, 1890, pronounced the book brilliant, "an altogether exceptional work . . . masterful in construction
and scholarly in execution"; the *New York Tribune* called
it "an honor to the author and to the United States Navy
he so well serves."[4] The book was reviewed throughout
Europe, and particularly widely in England, where Mahan had many disciples; Kaiser Wilhelm claimed that

every German naval vessel had a copy on board; the Japanese translated the book in 1897.

The book actually was the first volume of a trilogy. In 1892 the second volume, *The Influence of Sea Power upon the French Revolution and Empire, 1793–1812,* was published to equally appreciative reviews. The third volume, which Mahan considered his best but about which the public was less enthusiastic, was published in 1905. Between the second and third volumes Mahan wrote a two-volume biography of Lord Nelson, and after he completed the Sea Power series he published several collections of articles and lectures, all of which were produced by Little, Brown.

A parsimonious man, counting every penny of his royalties and overjoyed when the check was larger than he expected, Mahan wrote nothing for which he was not paid. The first two Sea Power books earned him some five thousand dollars between 1891 and 1895, a considerable sum in those days. Even more important was his influence on the political thought of his time. His books were used as authoritative texts by both the Allies and the Germans in World War I and are still read today.

The works of Sienkiewicz, Farmer, and Mahan opened new vistas for Little, Brown and introduced it to the world of competitive trade publishing. The next move, the purchase of Roberts Brothers, greatly expanded the firm and made it at last a major trade publishing house.

8

Thomas Niles and His Firm

When Little, Brown purchased Roberts Brothers in 1898 and added more than nine hundred titles to its list, it was profiting from the labors and good judgment of the remarkable Thomas Niles, Jr.

Niles began his career in a not too dissimilar fashion from the way the nineteenth-century partners at Little, Brown started theirs. He was born in Boston in 1825, attended Boston Latin School, and at the age of fourteen went to work as a clerk at William D. Ticknor's Old Corner Bookstore. Here he made friends with another clerk, James T. Fields, who would become Ticknor's partner in 1854. The two young men profited from the excellent training they received from Ticknor himself. Niles was soon put in charge of the firm's correspondence, a position that gave him a close-up view of the subtleties of bookselling and managing author relations. He also benefited from his acquaintance with the notables who passed through Ticknor's doors: Emerson, Hawthorne, Whittier, Prescott, Lowell, and Louis Agassiz were all

frequent visitors. By 1855 Niles decided to strike out on
his own as a book publisher. Shy, somewhat taciturn,
Niles was nevertheless ambitious and desirous of greater
opportunity than clerkship offered.

His first venture was as a partner in Whittemore, Niles
and Hall, located on Washington Street a few doors
down from Ticknor and Fields. The new firm was making a modest start in publishing poetry, fiction, and children's books, but it was not strong enough to survive the
panic of 1857, and in 1858 the partnership was dissolved.
Then in 1863 Niles seized the opportunity to join a firm
established by Lewis Roberts and his brother, Austin,
only two years earlier. Roberts Brothers was doing a
profitable business selling photograph albums, which
became popular during the Civil War. To be sure, photograph albums did not seem to offer much promise for
future successful trade publishing, nor did the rampant
inflation of 1863, brought about by the war. Still, Lewis
Roberts offered Niles the chance to publish books, and
the first Roberts Brothers list was announced in the
American Publishers Circular and Literary Gazette of August 1,
1863.

The list was a modest one, some of the titles having already been published by the recently dissolved New
York firm of C. S. Francis and Company, but already
there was an emphasis on juvenile literature, which was
to grow into an important part of Roberts Brothers'
publications. Niles's first great success, however, came
with that staple of nineteenth-century publishing, British poetry.

Practically no one today remembers the name of Jean
Ingelow, although a few (Bartlett's owners among them)

may vaguely recollect her best-known poem, "High Tide on the Coast of Lincolnshire 1571." At the time she was immensely popular in England, and Niles, after reading glowing reviews of her work in the British press, divined that her simple, sentimental poems about love, religion, children, and rural life would strike a responsive chord in America. He announced that Ingelow's work would be available in the United States under the Roberts Brothers imprint. Appleton of New York, which had also made such an announcement, gave way under courtesy of the trade. Niles's instinct was right: Ingelow's poems, published in October 1863, were an instant success. In five years twenty-five thousand copies were sold, and the profits from this one venture assured the early success of the new firm.

Ingelow also wrote a children's book, *Mopsa the Fairy*, published with some success by Roberts in 1869. Boston publishers in the 1860s were putting out a large number of what they called children's books. But the books were really moral or religious tracts in disguise, and the Civil War had added a strong dose of one-sided patriotism. So stereotyped, unnatural, and unchildlike was this juvenile "literature" that it had little appeal for its intended audience. The prescient Thomas Niles realized that children's books deserved special treatment and a fresh approach. As early as 1864 he successfully published *The Tanner Boy: And How He Became Lieutenant General*, a biography of Ulysses S. Grant, and *Pigeon Pie: A Tale of Roundhead Times* by the best-selling English romantic novelist Charlotte M. Yonge (both books were still in print and on the list that went to Little, Brown in 1898). Niles's greatest success, however, was still to come.

In the fall of 1867 a young woman from Concord, Massachusetts, came to Niles for consultation about what to write. Louisa May Alcott was by no means an inexperienced writer; in one way or another she had published a variety of material, mostly potboilers and romantic thrillers, for the last fifteen years. Bronson Alcott, Louisa's improvident, idealistic father, had kept the family in genteel poverty with a variety of philanthropic schemes, and Louisa had been working for years to support the family and rid it of the never-ending burden of debts. Now thirty-five, she had had one real success with *Hospital Sketches*, published in 1863 and based on her experiences as a nurse during the Civil War.

Niles, with his interest in juvenile literature, urged her to try her hand at a "girl's story," for which he felt the market was ripe. Encouraged by her family and by Niles's continued importunities, Louisa set to work in the spring of 1868, finishing the manuscript in July. Niles found the first chapters a little dull (so, for that matter, did Louisa), but the publisher gave the whole book to his young niece and her friends for an expert reading. Their reaction was overwhelmingly favorable.

The first volume of *Little Women* was published on October 1, 1868. The first printing, two thousand copies, sold out immediately, and the presses could hardly keep up with the subsequent demand. Louisa noted in her journal, "Mr. N. wants a second volume for Spring." He got it. Writing at the speed of a chapter a day, she brought the sequel to Niles on New Year's Day, 1869, and it was published on April 14. Thirteen thousand copies of the combined book sold out in two weeks. By year's end thirty-eight thousand copies had been sold,

and the book was well on its way to making the $200,000
its author is said to have earned from it. Niles had offered to pay Louisa $1,000 for the copyright but at the
same time advised her, as a friend, to keep the copyright
and accept royalties instead. "An honest publisher and
lucky author," Louisa later wrote in her diary, for the
coyright ownership made her fortune.[1]

Little Women made Roberts Brothers' fortune, too. The
importance of Louisa May Alcott to the firm cannot be
overemphasized, for the profit from her books alone was
enough to ensure its well-being. Not only did they sweep
the U.S. market, but they were also enormously popular
in England. Meanwhile, Niles and his best-known author developed a special friendship:

> After Niles had become acquainted with Louisa, the re-
> lationship between them developed into a personal
> friendship. . . . He kept strict watch on Louisa's style,
> often telling her specifically how to write, what to avoid,
> and what to strive for, and he was full of appreciation of
> her hard-won successes. A quiet, unaggressive man, he
> was a real influence on her work and a partner in her
> achievements.[2]

Niles went on to add other successful children's books
to the Roberts Brothers list. From England came Juliana
Horatia Ewing's *Lob-lie-by-the-Fire, The Brownies and Other
Stories*, and *Jackanapes*, one of the most popular of Victo-
rian nursery tales, illustrated by the famous Randolph
Caldecott. Also from England came Edward Lear's non-
sense books with his own illustrations. American authors
included Laura E. Richards, daughter of Julia Ward
Howe, whose charming verses Niles first published and
Little, Brown reissued under the title *Tirra-Lirra* in 1932,

when the author was eighty-two; Lucretia P. Hale, sister of Edward Everett Hale, whose *Last of the Peterkins* continued the saga of the wacky Peterkin family; and Mary P. Wells Smith, who began her Young Puritan series under the auspices of Roberts Brothers, although the entire Old Deerfield series was to be Little, Brown's publication. Matching *Little Women* in lasting acclaim if not in initial sales was Robert Louis Stevenson's *Treasure Island*, which Niles brought out in 1884.

By now Niles, who had been a partner in 1872, was the only visible head of a solidly successful firm, for Lewis Roberts, content with his photograph albums and his share of the profits of Niles's enterprise, had receded more and more into the background, so that outsiders doubted he even existed. The *American Literary Gazette* described the company:

> It is only just to say that the firm of Roberts Brothers are as fairly distinguished for their courteous and honorable business habits, as for their good taste and sound judgment, as displayed in the selection of books for the public. Their liberality to authors is proverbial; and their reputation in England, among writers and publishers, is as high as that of any American publishing house. An authoritative critic once remarked that there was not a single book on Roberts Brothers' list which he did not covet for his library — an opinion which will be cordially endorsed by the American public.[3]

The successes of Roberts Brothers were by no means confined to the juvenile field. Niles was a superb interpreter of America's literary tastes, a brilliant editor who was also gifted with considerable advertising skills and a flair for selling books. Works by Christina Rossetti, Algernon Charles Swinburne, and George Sand found their way onto his list, to be followed by those of Honoré de Balzac, whose works had been virtually unknown in the United States until Roberts Brothers published the excellent translations by Katharine Prescott Wormeley; and of George Meredith, whose reputation in Great Britain was greatly strengthened by the Roberts Brothers publication.

Nor did Niles neglect American authors. Among them were Edward Everett Hale, who had become well known in the 1860s for his short novel *The Man Without a Country*; and Helen Hunt Jackson, whose *Ramona* was published in 1884. *Ramona*, which brought about a marked change in the attitudes of whites toward Native Americans, was a very popular novel, selling more than a hundred thousand copies in its first ten years and continuing to sell for many decades. Mary W. Tileston's *Daily Strength for Daily Needs*, a selection of brief prose and verse passages interspersed with biblical quotations, was also published in 1884. By 1940 more than four hundred thousand copies had been sold, and the book is still in print and on the Little, Brown list today.

It was through Helen Hunt Jackson that Niles became the publisher of another writer whose reputation today probably outshines that of any other on the Roberts Brothers list. Mrs. Jackson, a friend of the reclusive Emily Dickinson, submitted one of Dickinson's poems to Niles for inclusion in an anthology the publisher was preparing. Niles was unenthusiastic but respected Mrs. Jackson's judgment and published it in *A Masque of Poets* in 1878.[4]

The story of the discovery of the nearly two thousand

Thomas Niles

Louisa May Alcott

Helen Hunt Jackson

Emily Dickinson

poems Emily Dickinson had written during her lifetime
and their editing is well known. It is to Thomas Niles's
credit that he recognized their worth and published the
first collection in 1890. Sixteen printings attested to his
good judgment; meanwhile, he published a second volume of Dickinson's poems in 1891 and, three years later,
The Letters of Emily Dickinson.

In the mid-1880s Roberts Brothers moved from Washington Street to Somerset Street, at the top of Beacon
Hill, into quarters as plain as their original ones had
been. Niles, although a considerate and respected em-
ployer, endorsed the old, Spartan New England virtues.
Everyone in the company — only seven employees —
was expected to work hard and long. Niles himself had
never taken a vacation. In 1894, at the age of sixty-nine,
he finally decided to take his first trip and died, sadly, in
Perugia, Italy. The shy, kind, talented man had made his
mark on publishing; said *Publishers Weekly:*

> He magnified his office by making it a truly literary
> function, and he had no stronger desire than to add good
> names to his very choice catalogue, to publish the best
> books, and to see that the authors of them receive their
> due reward. His warmest friends were among his au-
> thors, and in their mutual relations all traditions of dis-
> trust were set aside.[5]

Niles's death was a mortal blow to the firm. Lewis
Roberts tried to carry on, but he had no book publishing
talent or experience and was brusque and difficult with
his employees. The firm limped along for four years, reprinting books from back lists and occasionally publishing new volumes from Niles's authors, but the creative

genius had gone. In 1898 the publishing trade and the public learned, with some grief but no surprise, that the respected firm had been bought by Little, Brown.

And thus Little, Brown acquired that distinguished list. James McIntyre and John Murray Brown were delighted — so much so that for that Christmas they ordered a ton of coal to be placed in the cellar of each male employee who headed a household.

9

New Ventures,
1900–1925

James McIntyre was admitted to partnership at Little, Brown in 1897, joining senior partner John Murray Brown and Charles W. Allen, who had come to the firm from Ticknor and Fields in 1869 and who managed the finances. Following the acquisition of Roberts Brothers, the partners began to build on the firmly established trade-book base. Other cookbooks soon followed Fannie Farmer's, the success of *Quo Vadis* attracted more writers of fiction, and the outstanding children's books from Roberts Brothers provided an impetus for Little, Brown to develop its efforts in this field.

So did the market. The first decade of the twentieth century saw a tremendous upsurge in the publishing of books for children; publishers, authors, and titles were plentiful. Series books had a great appeal, and favorite authors were encouraged to produce at least a book a year. Among the most popular and productive authors published by Little, Brown were Susan Coolidge, Lily F. Wesselhoeft, A. G. Plympton, and Mary P. Wells Smith,

and of course the books by Louisa May Alcott continued
to lead the field. By far the most prolific author to publish with Little, Brown was Thornton W. Burgess.

Burgess, a native of Cape Cod, was working as an associate editor for *Good Housekeeping* in Springfield, Massachusetts, when an editorial representative of Little,
Brown happened to visit the magazine and the editor in
chief mentioned that Burgess wrote stories for children.
The representative read them, liked them, urged Burgess
to put them together as a possible book and send them
off to Boston, and "the unbelievable happened," said
Burgess. "I had signed a contract that would make me a
bona fide author. It was for *Old Mother West Wind.*"[1] The
book sold 2,100 copies in 1910, its first year, and Little,
Brown, pleased with this success, encouraged Burgess to
continue. He did so, going on to write more than sixty
books, many of them grouped as series. Total sales of
Burgess's books for children to date have been more than
7½ million; *Old Mother West Wind* is still in print.

Meanwhile, the firm was addressing the adolescent
reader. There were girls' books, such as *Sidney: Her Senior
Year, Frolics at Fairmount, A Prairie Rose*, and *The Wide
Awake Girls at College.* The boys enjoyed *Scouting for Light-
Horse Harry, Donald Kirk, the Morning Record Correspondent,
Henley on the Battle Line*, and *The Fourth Down.* These were
sweet, romantic, moral books; many were about school or
about orphans who made good. They were not too dissimilar from the adult books of the day.

From 1900 until shortly after World War I, the list at
Little, Brown featured a great deal of sentimental and
romantic fiction. It took the shock of the war to wean the
general reader away from this type of book and intro-

duce a stronger note of realism into popular literature. Most of these books were written by women whose names today are largely forgotten but who made a decided impress upon the reading world. A typical example is *Truth Dexter* by Sidney McCall (nom de plume of Mary McNeill Fenollosa), which the *St. Paul Globe* described as a record of "the life of a pure woman whose every thought, word, or action is love of both mankind and nature. . . . As a character study of all that a woman should or may be, the heroine, Truth Dexter, embodies all these human attributes." *Truth Dexter* sold some forty thousand copies within a year of its publication. The comparison with the romance fiction of the 1980s is inevitable; escapism knows no time or place.

Not all of Little, Brown's female authors were writing fiction, yet the themes were not unalike. Annie Payson Call wrote an inspirational book called *The Freedom of Life*, about which the *St. Louis Globe Democrat* said, "Those who are afflicted with overwork, with insomnia, with damaged nerve power of any kind will find the simplest and most available methods for bettering their condition." *The Chicago Chronicle* called Lilian Whiting's *The Life Radiant* "a clear perception of the meaning of life and of the infinite possibilities of the human soul."

And not all of Little, Brown's authors were women; there were men, and furthermore, the men were writing romances, if a little more stalwart and adventuresome than Truth Dexter's saga. Jeffery Farnol, for example, told the story of a young Englishman during the eighteenth century who ventures off on foot rather than comply with the terms of his eccentric uncle's will in the immensely popular *Broad Highway*, published in 1911 and selling 180,000 copies. Farnol became a perennial best-seller and wrote thirty-six books during his lifetime. A.S.M. Hutchinson's *Happy Warrior* figured well on the 1913 list; the London *Post* called it "a book in a million."

Probably the author Little, Brown was most grateful for was E. Phillips Oppenheim, writer of popular thrillers, who began publishing with the company in 1903 and consistently thereafter wrote two or three novels a year. Over a sixty-year period Little, Brown published 134 of his novels. The best known is undoubtedly *The Great Impersonation*, which came out in 1920. There was some speculation as to how Oppenheim actually produced his novels, since he was seldom seen writing. He would spend his daytimes playing golf, and only a few cognoscenti knew that he dictated his works to a secretary in the early evenings.

In April 1908 the redoubtable John Murray Brown, having served the firm for forty-five years, died suddenly of pneumonia. Thereupon James McIntyre became senior partner, and it was not long before he decided to move the firm from the Washington Street location it had had for seventy-two years.

Not only had Little, Brown changed, so also had Washington Street. Once frequented by the knowledgeable and the book-loving, it had become an area now populated by commercial vendors and cheap restaurants — the generally more graceless denizens of a less intellectual environment. McIntyre found a handsome house at 34 Beacon Street available and ideally suited for the expanding firm.

This lovely house had been built on property originally owned by John Hancock, that dashing signer of the

Declaration of Independence. Completed in 1826, it had first been lived in by Nathaniel Pope Russell, had been sold after his death to James Bowdoin Bradlee, and had then come into the hands of Susan B. Cabot of Salem in 1878. One of a trio of houses gracing the summit of Beacon Hill, it overlooked the Boston Common in its sweep from the State House down to Tremont Street.

Although constructed as a private residence, the house needed little alteration to serve as the home of a publisher and bookseller. The high-ceilinged rooms were large and airy; the carved woodwork and beautiful marble fireplaces in many of the rooms were classically elegant. Some of the walls were left with their tapestries in place, while others displayed original art from the large stock of illustrations Little, Brown had commissioned for its books from the leading artists of the day.

The retail shop was set up on the first floor in what had formerly been the downstairs sitting room, where it remained until the company finally gave up the retail-book business in 1921. The first floor also housed the law-book sales rooms. The front portion of the second floor was devoted, as it still is, to offices — some with French windows opening onto a small iron-grilled balcony facing the Common — for the managers of the firm. The rest of the second floor housed the editorial and advertising departments, while the manufacturing and art departments were located on the third floor, along with a sample room for visitors. The growing schoolbook and subscription departments were on the fourth floor, and the fifth was used for storage. A handsome entrance was graced by clipped boxwood trees placed just inside the front door and a stained-glass panel in the inner door. Close behind the building was a connected annex, which was used for the wholesale and shipping departments.

James McIntyre did not enjoy Little, Brown's new home for very long; in 1913 he, too, died of pneumonia. A believer in providing the company with standard works as well as lighter fiction, he had kept many of the classics on the list at the same time that he had steered the expansion into more general works. He himself had spent nearly ten years exercising editorial control over Richard Grant White's new, eighteen-volume edition of Shakespeare and putting great effort into searching out and editing the uncollected letters of Daniel Webster, which were published in three volumes in 1902. Known to all for his good nature and fair dealing, he was sorely missed by booksellers and publishers around the country. Happily, he lived long enough to see his only son, Alfred McIntyre, join the firm in 1907 upon his graduation from Harvard.

Upon McIntyre's death there was a change in the structure of Little, Brown. Its growth made a partnership now inappropriate, so the firm became incorporated under the leadership of Charles W. Allen, its first president. The editorial department became the responsibility of Herbert F. Jenkins, who had joined the company in 1901, and Alfred R. McIntyre; Allen retained his financial role. The corporation was set up so that shares of its stock were available only to employees. Stock ownership was encouraged and cut across all levels; the janitor and the president both owned shares. Thus ownership was retained by the firm, for if an employee owning stock left the company, he or she was required to sell it back to Little, Brown.

Under the new management the kinds of books pub-

James W. McIntyre

Thornton W. Burgess

E. Phillips Oppenheim

Charles W. Allen

lished, for the most part, changed very little. Romance was still the mainstay of the adult list, buttressed by history, travel, cooking, and inspirational books. Westerns became very popular; it was something of a shock to find out that the prolific B. M. Bower, who wrote many a rough-and-tough western, was really a woman. Some new projects were the Mind and Health series, which dealt with the interrelationship of bodily and mental states in the causation and cure of disease, and an extensive series on drama. The success of Little, Brown's children's books had led the firm in 1904 to establish the schoolbook department, which specialized in publishing supplementary readers and soon expanded to include textbooks in domestic science (what we now call home economics).

World War I did not see any remarkable change in the type of books published, although there were a number of war-related volumes: Annie Payson Call's *Nerves and the War*; *A Yankee in the Trenches* by R. D. Holmes; *Letters of a Canadian Stretcher Bearer*, edited by Anna Chapin Ray; and Jeffery Farnol's *Great Britain at War*. If anything, escapism became more popular and whodunits began to appear regularly. We find such titles as *The Chinese Label*, *The La Chance Mine Mystery*, and *The Mystery at Ritsmore* on the lists from the war decade.

Best-sellers were gratifyingly present. In 1921 the firm published A.S.M. Hutchinson's *If Winter Comes*, a turbulent novel that dealt with illegitimacy and divorce, and in 1925 the top fiction title, A. Hamilton Gibbs's *Soundings*. Charles Warren's *The Supreme Court in United States History* was awarded the Pulitzer Prize for history in 1923, and Owen Davis's *Icebound* the prize for the best

American play in the same year. What is interesting about the best-sellers during the decades of the teens and twenties is that most of the male fiction authors were British and most of the female authors American, whereas in the nonfiction line authors generally were Americans.

It can be said generally that diversity of subject matter prevailed at this time. In 1920, for instance, the adult reader could choose *The Colonial Architecture of Philadelphia* or *The Nervous Housewife*; *A Guide to the Military History of the World War* or *Black Bartlemy's Treasure*. Girls could read *Her Book: A Story of Sweet Sixteen* by Anna Chapin Ray; boys could turn to *An American Boy at Henley* by Frank E. Channon. Children's books, law books, history books, and the ever-present light fiction prevailed.

Once again, it was time for a change. In 1925 that change, as important to the company as the purchase of Roberts Brothers twenty-seven years before, came about.

10

The Expansive Twenties

O ne day toward the end of 1924 Alfred McIntyre and
Mark A. DeWolfe Howe, associate editor of the
Atlantic Monthly, met on the train from Boston to New
York. In the relaxed atmosphere of the parlor car their
talk turned to business. The prestigious *Atlantic Monthly*
was owned by Ellery Sedgwick, who had bought it from
Houghton Mifflin Company in 1908 and had started the
publication of a select list of books in 1917. Many of
these books, Howe admitted, languished unsold in the
Atlantic's warehouse, not because they had been badly
chosen but because the fledgling Atlantic Monthly Press
did not have a large enough marketing force to get them
to the booksellers.

Howe and McIntyre began to discuss how their re-
spective companies might work together. It was natural
enough to consider some kind of partnership: The two
firms were geographically close, with the *Atlantic*'s offices
and warehouse only a half-mile away from Little,
Brown's, on Arlington Street facing the Public Garden.

Little, Brown was a mature and experienced publishing house, with a list of great vitality and a strong, efficient organization for manufacturing and selling books. The Atlantic Monthly Press in nearly eight years had published some 125 titles, many of which were notable, and had the advantage of its connection with the magazine. The *Atlantic Monthly*, founded in 1857, attracted contributions from the leading writers of the day, many of whom were disposed to look favorably on the company's book-publishing arm. It seemed a very clear opportunity for both firms. When McIntyre returned to Boston, he arranged a meeting with Ellery Sedgwick.

Sedgwick, not only the owner of the company but also its president and editor of the magazine, immediately recognized the advantages of a Little, Brown connection, and an agreement was reached. Before it became final, Arthur H. Thornhill, Sr., one of McIntyre's most knowledgeable and experienced salesmen, was asked to assess the Atlantic Monthly Press stock in hand; he recommended selling off a large part of the excess.

On February 26, 1925, it was agreed that Little, Brown and the Atlantic Monthly Press would work together to publish Atlantic–Little, Brown books. Under the terms of the agreement, the books were to be developed editorially at the Atlantic, a joint decision of the two companies would be made as to which books would be published, and Little, Brown would copyedit, manufacture, and sell the Atlantic titles. Little, Brown was responsible for financing, paying the Atlantic royalties for all copies sold, and each title published in this manner was to bear the Atlantic–Little, Brown imprint. All past, present, and future Atlantic books were to be included as

long as the agreement was in effect, which initially was
for a period of five years.

Sedgwick was pleased to announce the new arrangement to his authors. On February 20, 1925, for example,
he wrote to John Jay Chapman:

> Dear Jack,
> The enclosed announcement tells you of a step we are
> making here which we believe is greatly to the advantage
> of our authors and ourselves. Atlantic books will con-
> tinue to have all the advantages, editorial and other,
> which we have been able to give them. They will be se-
> lected, edited and designed for the press by us. They will
> be published and sold by an organization half a dozen
> times as big as we could afford to create for our small se-
> lected list. We have all liked the attitude of Little, Brown
> & Company during the negotiations, and I believe your
> book will profit definitely by association with them.[1]

During the previous eight years the Atlantic Monthly
Press had published many outstanding books, among
them two Pulitzer Prize–winners, James Truslow
Adams's *The Founding of New England* and *Barrett Wendell
and His Letters* by Mark A. DeWolfe Howe; a series of sea
stories for children by Charles Boardman Hawes, the last
of which, *The Dark Frigate*, won the Newbery Medal for
1923; and *The Letters of William James*, edited by his son,
Henry. The press maintained a small list, striving for excellence in a few fields, such as biography, history, belles
lettres, and juvenile literature. Its staff was correspond-
ingly small; apart from Sedgwick and Donald Snyder,
assistant publisher, its most important member was Edward Weeks, who had joined the company in 1924 and
was to have a long and distinguished career with it,

working, like Sedgwick, on both the books and the magazine.

On Little, Brown's side, the architect of this significant development in the company's history was Alfred McIntyre. Very different in personality and physique from his father, James McIntyre, he shared the older man's love of books, intelligence, and desire to excel. James had been stocky, outgoing, largely self-educated; Alfred was slight, high-strung, a graduate of Harvard. In one generation the McIntyres had produced a scion who seemed the epitome of the Beacon Hill patrician. Alfred's personality, however, by no means included a disdain for work. He started at Little, Brown directly after his graduation from Harvard in 1907 and worked in all departments of the company, getting a thorough grounding in both the business and the creative sides of publishing. In 1911 he became a partner, and in 1913, when the company was incorporated, general manager. After serving in France during World War I as a regimental sergeant major in the 301st Infantry, he returned to Little, Brown as vice-president and general manager, and was named the second president in 1926.

McIntyre's first years as president were marked on the whole by productivity and commercial and artistic success. The emphases of the list had changed dramatically after ninety years. By 1928 the law books, once so important, accounted for only 7 percent of the company's sales. The lion's share, 65 percent, came from trade books; educational publishing made up 14 percent, and the remainder was provided by direct sales and the company bindery. Retail bookselling ended in 1921.

Little, Brown moved ahead decisively in publishing

both plays and books connected with the theater. There were plays by the Quintero brothers, the leading Spanish dramatists; by Arthur Schnitzler; by Harley Granville-Barker; and by George Kelly, whose *Craig's Wife* won the 1926 Pulitzer Prize for the best American play of 1925. Numerous anthologies of plays (including plays for children) appeared, as did theatrical autobiographies and reminiscences such as Konstantin Stanislavski's *My Life in Art* and *Up the Years from Bloomsbury* by George Arliss.

From the Atlantic Monthly Press came a steady flow of quality works — biography, history, the controversial *Case of Sacco and Vanzetti* by Felix Frankfurter. To encourage new writers, the Atlantic set up several prize contests, among them ten thousand dollars for the best work of fiction. The first winner of this prize in 1927 was Mazo de la Roche, whose novel *Jalna* not only was a runaway best-seller but also initiated a whole series, deservedly popular, about the lives and loves of a clannish British family isolated on a country estate in Canada. Some of the Jalna books are still in print.

Many of the changes taking place in American society during the 1920s had a favorable impact upon the publishing industry. The first commercial radio broadcast was made in 1920; by 1930 some 40 percent of American homes owned at least one radio. Here was a new medium that could publicize writers' works and also dramatize them. The development of motion pictures from a curiosity to a national passion opened up another medium and market, for a successful book could go on to become a successful film, which in turn would lead the public back to the book. The trend toward apartment living and smaller houses, where people had less space for books, led to an increase in the number of lending libraries and rental sections in bookstores.

The most important changes, however, from a publisher's point of view, were the growth of the size of the reading public and the creation of book clubs. In 1890 only 6 percent of fourteen- to seventeen-year-olds had attended high school; in 1928 more than 40 percent had. Thus there was a considerably wider and more diversified reading audience. In April 1926 the Book-of-the-Month Club was launched as a means "to distribute the best *new* books being published — books that would be chosen by an independent and eminent board of literary experts, books that would be sent through the mail across the country."[2] Clearly, it was an idea whose time had come; the club was successful from the start. The Literary Guild was begun in 1927, and thereafter book clubs have proliferated. Their effect upon publishing has been profound.

Two in-house changes that would be important for the future of Little, Brown also took place in the 1920s. One was the creation of a separate children's book department; the other was the establishment of a trade department office in New York. Originally this was no more than an outpost of the trade sales department, staffed by a single sales representative whose job was to look after the big New York buyers, such as the American News Company. Later, the office grew to include first a trade editor to keep in touch with New York literary agents and eventually other representatives of the trade editorial, sales, and publicity departments.

From time to time in American history some sections of the population take it upon themselves to legislate so-

cial values and force the entire nation to conform to their
system of morality. The twenties was such a period. It
was the decade of Prohibition and also the decade of a
determined effort to censor books. This movement was
particularly strong in Boston. In New York the Sumner
Society for the Suppression of Vice seized books and took
their publishers to court. In Boston the Watch and Ward
Society acted against booksellers. When the society believed that a book violated Massachusetts obscenity laws,
it warned the owners of the bookstores, and in most cases
booksellers simply refused to stock the book. Little,
Brown, like other publishers, of course was affected by
these actions. In 1927 Little, Brown and the Atlantic
spoke out jointly against local censorship in the case of
Upton Sinclair's *Oil!*, even though that book had not
been published by them. The officers of the firms wrote:

> As citizens concerned with public decency and the main-
> tenance of public sanity, as publishers associated during
> the active lifetime of all of us with books and magazines
> of honorable reputations, we wish publicly and seriously
> to protest against the high-handed, erratic, and ill-
> advised interference of certain public officials with the
> sale and distribution of books, many of them of recog-
> nized standing and freely sold elsewhere throughout the
> United States. . . . It is difficult for men of self-respect to
> keep silence in the face of this violation of the historic
> tradition of Boston and New England.[3]

Oil! survived the Watch and Ward Society, and so did
Webster's Dictionary, which had been attacked by a Boston
city councilman for being pro-British. As the famous
cases regarding *Ulysses* and *Lady Chatterley's Lover* attest,
censorship survived as well, affecting Little, Brown's

Alfred R. McIntyre

Erich Maria Remarque

publication of one of the most notable novels of the entire decade, Erich Maria Remarque's *All Quiet on the Western Front.*

Perhaps the best known of the antiwar novels published in the wake of World War I, *All Quiet on the Western Front* spoke for a generation. Thirty-one when he wrote it, Remarque had been conscripted into the German army at eighteen and sent to the western front. Here he was wounded five times; his friends were killed all around him, and his mother died while he was away. Remarque returned home to a solitary, alienated existence that seemed to typify the fate of his fellow survivors, and he told their story in his powerful, starkly truthful portrayal of the horror and futility of war. It was a sensation in Germany, where five hundred thousand copies were sold in four months, and also in the English-speaking world. The London *Sunday Observer* said, "It is the most wonderful and terrible book that has come out of the war. Here is no glamour, no glory. At last the epic of the lowly soldier in the line, the true story of the world's greatest nightmare"; Christopher Morley in the *Saturday Review of Literature* summed it up as "the greatest book about the war which I have yet seen."

Little, Brown came to publish *All Quiet* because of the astuteness of Herbert Jenkins, the firm's editor in chief. Early in 1929 Jenkins told McIntyre that in his opinion a revival of interest in the war was about due. Not long after, he showed McIntyre an article in the London *Observer* about the current popularity of war novels in Germany. Among them was *Im Westen nichts Neues.* The short description of the book convinced the two men that they wanted it, and they cabled a London literary agent.

On March 4, 1929, Little, Brown succeeded in signing it up, thereby scooping another American publisher who had been interested but had not thought to cable.

The book was subsequently chosen by the Book-of-the-Month Club as its main selection, and their judges proposed several changes regarding offensive words and incidents, leaving it up to Little, Brown to act on them as it saw fit. One of the judges helpfully suggested that the offending words could be translated into Latin. Jenkins rejected that, but he knew, as he put it, that "some of the words and sentences were too robust for our American edition." Both Massachusetts and federal laws would prevent untrammeled selling or dispatch of the book by mail unless the changes were made. They were relatively unimportant; three words and five phrases were deleted, as well as two episodes. Years later, when censorship had become much less of a problem, the words and phrases were quietly restored without arousing comment.

One of the most widely read books of its period, *All Quiet on the Western Front* sold 3½ million copies in three years in the original German and was translated into more than twenty-five languages. It accounted for 20 percent of Little, Brown's trade sales in 1929, the year it was published, and became the number-one nationwide best-seller that year.

Altogether, the decade before the Great Depression was a profitable one for Little, Brown. The first five-year contract between the firm and the Atlantic Monthly Press had worked extremely well. Both sides had demonstrated their ability to offer a high level of professionalism, close cooperation, and basic friendship in a unique publishing arrangement. The contract was renewed with minor changes for another five years in 1930 and again in 1935 for still another five years. In 1941, so successful was the arrangement continuing to be that this time it was renewed for a fifty-year period.

11

Depression and Celebration

Non refert quam multos sed quam bonos habeas is the motto on Little, Brown's third colophon. Freely translated as "fewer and better books," this expresses one of Alfred McIntyre's deepest and most abiding convictions and was the guideline for Little, Brown during the difficult, Depression-ridden 1930s.

In an article entitled "Birth Control for Books," which appeared in the December 26, 1931, issue of *Publishers Weekly*, McIntyre argued the case for fewer books, speculating pessimistically on the prospects for the book industry in the coming year. His predictions proved correct. A drop in purchasing by the general public, increased use of libraries with simultaneous restrictions on buying by the libraries, and curtailment of school appropriations all meant smaller book sales in 1932.

Fortunately, McIntyre in 1929 had determined that list control was necessary, although his policies did not take full effect until 1931. Thus in 1930 Little, Brown published ninety-three new books, in 1931 sixty-seven, and sixty-five in 1932, which turned out to be the worst year of the Depression. In that year, for the first time in its existence, Little, Brown did not show a profit. Moreover, two pay cuts had been instituted, a third was under consideration, and no dividends were paid on the stock — a blow to the stockholders, all of whom were, of course, also employees. In his report to them early in 1933, McIntyre was, if anything, even more pessimistic.

> The Trade Department's back list books have almost stopped selling, with bookstores unwilling to stock them for lack of quick turnover and public libraries unable to buy them for lack of funds. . . . Appropriations for school books have been tremendously reduced and supplementary readers, always till now the major part of our Educational list, have suffered most; we are developing a college list, but it comes too late to take up the slack as yet. Lawyers are not buying, law school students must be using second-hand books. With heavy stocks of old books on hand, we can offer our Bindery almost solely new books to bind; it has been operating one unit three days a week instead of two units full time. Meanwhile fixed charges go on — heat, light, and telephone cost about as much as three years ago, real estate taxes and postage are higher.[1]

McIntyre's cost-cutting measures did, however, help see the firm through a period when many of its contemporaries foundered. In 1933 only 111 million copies of new books were printed throughout the United States, as compared with the more than 214 million printed in 1929.

McIntyre's dedication to "fewer and better" was actually a matter of general principle rather than merely one of immediate commercial expediency. He fervently believed that certain books should be published even if they were unprofitable, but that many second-rate and unprofitable books should not. Later, he liked to point out that despite the list restriction of the early thirties Little, Brown had turned down only one book that had done well on another publisher's list, and that was a novel by an author whose previous book had been a failure.

Even in so difficult a commercial climate, Little, Brown and the Atlantic Monthly Press managed to publish a good many outstanding titles. They included the war memoirs of David Lloyd George, *Napoleon* by Jacques Bainville, and the memoirs of Prince Bernhard von Bülow, which gave an insider's view of the workings of the German government from the time of Bismarck to World War I. From the Atlantic came *The Epic of America* by James Truslow Adams and Bennett Champ Clark's *John Quincy Adams: Old Man Eloquent.* The Atlantic fiction prize for 1932 was won by Ann Bridges (a pseudonym for Lady Mary Dolling O'Malley) for her *Peking Picnic.* Another Atlantic triumph in that year was *Mutiny on the Bounty*, the classic tale by Charles Nordhoff and James Norman Hall. These two men were admirable collaborators, with Nordhoff drawing the broad strokes and Hall filling in the details of nuance and style. Edward Weeks, who was fond of both, felt each man's talents complemented the other's perfectly.

Many mysteries appeared during these years, as well as popular novels by the durable Jeffery Farnol, Mazo de la Roche, A.S.M. Hutchinson, and A. Hamilton Gibbs. Books with a "message" also were popular. Perhaps it was the general disenchantment with worldly values that prompted the great Atlantic–Little, Brown success of 1934, James Hilton's *Good-bye, Mr. Chips.* The well-known story of how Hilton came to write it is worth retelling.

One day in the fall of 1933 Hilton happened to meet the editor of the *British Weekly* in a London street. The man offered to pay the considerable sum of fifty pounds for a Christmas story, provided Hilton could deliver it in two weeks. Hilton agreed, even though he was dismayed by the shortness of the time, and then went through the torture so many authors experience — his imagination simply refused to produce. Finally, panic-stricken, he took his bicycle and pedaled off into the countryside, determined not to return until a plot came to him. "It was only at the end of the day as he was returning that the happy conception of Mr. Chips came to his mind. That evening he went to his typewriter, and in four days the story was written."[2]

"Good-bye, Mr. Chips" was duly published in the *British Weekly* and caught the eye of Ellery Sedgwick. He bought it for the *Atlantic Monthly*, and it was so well received that Sedgwick urged its publication as a small book. Hilton was willing to sell it outright in order to pay for a vacation in Switzerland, but Alfred McIntyre, well known for his generosity to authors, would have none of that. Cabling Hilton to reject this unwise course, McIntyre advanced enough money for Hilton's vacation and as well offered him a good contract. Hilton's whole world was changed by that fortuitous bicycle ride, and McIntyre's magnanimity was rewarded, for Hilton went on to write several Atlantic–Little, Brown best-sellers.

The tide of the Depression was beginning to turn in

1934 for the publishing industry. Little, Brown published *Brinkley Manor* by P. G. Wodehouse, and the Atlantic rounded off the *Bounty* trilogy with *Men Against the Sea* and *Pitcairn's Island*. Profits began to creep up, greatly assisted by the sale of a hundred thousand dollars' worth of Atlantic Readers, the Atlantic Monthly Press's line of educational storybooks, to the state of Oklahoma. By year's end in 1935, Little, Brown was able to report its best year since the Depression began. Two books that later became successful films were published that year: *My Man Godfrey* by Eric Hatch and *The African Queen* by C. S. Forester. The Atlantic's *Rats, Lice and History* by the eminent microbiologist Hans Zinsser made the story of typhus so exciting that the book became a classic and is still in print.

Also still in print is Walter D. Edmonds's *Drums Along the Mohawk*, the Atlantic–Little, Brown best-seller of 1936. The story of how its title came to be was told by Edward Weeks, by that point the director of the Atlantic Monthly Press, in an article in the *Saturday Review of Literature*:

> We were struggling together once for the right title for a new novel by Walter Edmonds, a novel describing the fortitude and misery of the colonists in the Mohawk Valley at the time of the American Revolution. Walter, as I remember, had called his story, *A Starving Wilderness*, which was not exactly an inviting title for the depression. Alfred, as he fingered through the manuscript, said, "These people lived in the Mohawk Valley. 'Mohawk' is a good word." Pause. "How did the news of the Revolution first reach them?" "Why," I said, "I guess it was when they first heard the drums of the Continentals."

"Drums," he said. "*Drums on the Mohawk*. No, you need more movement — *Drums Along the Mohawk*." And there was the title.[3]

This charming anecdote not only illustrates how closely the Atlantic and Little, Brown worked together but also gives a clear insight into Alfred McIntyre's personality and acumen. In the same article Weeks went on to describe the man who had so successfully shepherded Little, Brown through the past difficult years:

> He was slender, remarkably erect and wiry . . . diffident, painfully so; yet it was his daily ordeal to screw up his moral courage and walk out of his shyness to be his forthright self. . . . As you came to know him, you watched his hands. They were thin fingered and at times more expressive than his words. . . . He was not given much to handshaking or shoulder patting. But his hands talked. . . . With his tenacity went a friendliness, a friendliness deep and abiding despite his starched New England appearance. . . . Alfred McIntyre was the hardest fighter I have ever known in the book trade. He was a good trader and he loved to trade. But once the agreement was made, he stood by his promise to the full measure of his words and without deviation. . . . He believed that the purpose of publishing was to edify quite as much as to entertain, and that it was the courage of a publisher not to follow a party line, but to reconcile as far as books of ideas ever can the conservatism of the Right and the extravagances of the Left — in short, to find and publish the middle course, the American course.[4]

It was as much to honor this sophisticated, urbane, well-liked and admired man as well as the firm itself that many of McIntyre's authors and friends came to Boston

Little, Brown's One Hundredth Anniversary Dinner

C. S. Forester

Copley Plaza Hotel, Boston, March 31, 1937

Edward Weeks

John P. Marquand

from around the world in 1937 to celebrate Little, Brown's hundredth anniversary.

The oldest book publisher in Boston, Little, Brown could look back on its achievements with pride. Not only had it surmounted a series of financial stresses, slumps, and panics that had brought down many of its competitors, but also it had built a record of solid achievement in a variety of fields. Book sales were continuing to look up; 1937 was to prove the most successful year for Little, Brown since 1930. The company felt able to award itself a modest pat on the back:

> This is our centenary year. We may well be proud that we have weathered the depression (if it is over) with only one year failing to show some profit, and that throughout it we have been able to maintain our reputation for honesty and fair dealing and have not sought for immediate profit when the securing of it might weaken our future prospects.[5]

To honor the centennial, the *Saturday Review of Literature* included a special section about Little, Brown in its issue of March 27, 1937. Bernard De Voto headed the section with his article "Author and Publisher." In it he spoke affectionately and respectfully of Little, Brown as a firm that let him do his job as a writer without interference while expecting the same attitude from him in regard to the company's areas of expertise. De Voto recounted how editor Herbert Jenkins had offered him his first advance when he was working on *Mark Twain's America.* Needing some ready cash, De Voto had planned to put the book aside and earn some money writing articles; when Jenkins heard of this, he asked De Voto if a five-hundred-dollar advance would tide him over. "To be sure," wrote De Voto, "this was my first Little, Brown book but I had collaborated in the writing of two others and regarded myself as well informed. . . . [However,] I had never heard of an advance. If I have since become an addict, the firm has only itself to blame."

De Voto recalled the many pleasant hours he had spent at 34 Beacon Street and, with amusement, the cable that "Jenkins, a most moral man, had to send from London in order to list the expressions that had been deleted in the English edition of *Journey to the End of the Night*," Louis-Ferdinand Céline's earthy masterpiece of invective published in 1932. "One hopes," De Voto said, "that all cable clerks are male and world-weary." More seriously, De Voto added a vignette about Alfred McIntyre's reaction when informed that all eighty thousand words of *Mountain Time*, a De Voto novel that Little, Brown had already announced to the trade, had literally gone up the chimney. The dissatisfied De Voto had burned everything he had written so far. "All right," said McIntyre, and talked genially of other things. "If you can do that," De Voto wrote admiringly, "you are a publisher."

Christopher Morley, in his article "Bibliodisiacs," attributed Little, Brown's longevity to its true love of books, without which a publishing house is no more than a merchandiser. Said Morley:

> The most interesting thing (to me) in the history of Little, Brown is not its long roll of respected authors, nor its unblemished record of just, good-humored and canny trading, nor its domicile in the pure serene of Beacon Hill. It is the fact that it (and also its famous component,

Roberts Brothers, still honored in observance) was born out of a bookstore. . . . They would rather handle, read, and sell books than anything else in the world. Books to them were not just convenient packages of trade but that indescribable heat and excitement of the mind, that recognition in a stranger of one's own most precious or pitiful stirrings.

Certainly Morley expressed a philosophy still held by Little, Brown: that books are creations, to be admired, read, and sold, not anonymous and unvaried products; authors are the practitioners of an enormously demanding art and craft as well as the foundation of the entire publishing process.

In that same section of the *Saturday Review* the firm published a list of "One Hundred Books of Permanent Worth" that it had issued since 1900. The list for 1937 paled a little against the cream of the last thirty-six years, but it was nevertheless a strong one, containing a wide variety of books. Leading off was *Pedlar's Progress: The Life of Bronson Alcott* by Odell Shepard, which had won Little, Brown's centenary prize in competition with 368 manuscripts and went on to win a co-Pulitzer Prize for biography in 1938. The book was notable in making clear that Bronson Alcott, known chiefly as Louisa May Alcott's somewhat prodigal father, was in fact one of the most brilliant figures in New England intellectual history and a journal-keeper par excellence.

John P. Marquand had already published three of his popular Mr. Moto detective stories with Little, Brown; in 1937, the firm issued what was to be both one of Marquand's and Little, Brown's most important books, *The Late George Apley*. The book won the Pulitzer Prize in 1938, established Marquand's reputation as a serious novelist, and went on to become a classic of both the stage and the screen. Marquand was unsure of his venture and sought advice from Alfred McIntyre about it:

> I personally have enjoyed writing it, and think it is amusing, and think that it is a fairly accurate satire of Boston life. I certainly don't want to go ahead with the thing, however, if you don't think it holds any promise. . . . I know you will tell me frankly just how it strikes you, and its fate rests largely in your hands. Tell me quickly.

McIntyre thought the book might not be commercially successful, but he appreciated Marquand's desire to write a serious novel and replied sympathetically: "John, I personally think it is swell. I can't tell you whether it will sell more than 2,000 copies — it may be too highly specialized. But by all means go ahead with it."[6]

Another novelist who felt compelled to write something a little different was the Scottish author-physician A. J. Cronin. Little, Brown had already successfully published several of Cronin's earlier books, including the powerful *Hatter's Castle*, but *The Citadel* was something special. Wrote Cronin: "A little more than two months ago I was simply bowled over, knocked sideways, blown sky-high (any of these phrases will do!) by an obsession to write what is now turning out to be the most marvellous medical novel. . . . I am half way through and crazy about it. . . . I simply *HAD* to write this book!"[7] Again, McIntyre was encouraging and supportive. Published in 1937, *The Citadel* went straight to the top of the best-seller lists.

The year 1937 also marked the inception of a series

that has given immense pleasure to thousands of readers over the years when C. S. Forester's *Beat to Quarters*, the first novel about Captain Horatio Hornblower, that lively fictional hero of the Napoleonic wars, was published. The Hornblower series, recently reissued in paperback, is enchanting a whole new generation.

In the autumn of 1937 a landmark publication of the anniversary year appeared: the eleventh edition of *Bartlett's Familiar Quotations*. Nearly a quarter of a century had elapsed since the previous edition. The new editors, Christopher Morley and Louella D. Everett, had undertaken a massive revision. Out went many quotations that a new generation would no longer find "familiar"; in went twice as many as were dropped, the fruit of that twenty-five years of memorable uses of words and of the rise in public esteem of formerly neglected writers.

The firm also set up a novelette contest in honor of its hundredth birthday, believing that this shorter form of fiction would encourage many writers. The response was gratifying; 1,340 manuscripts were received. The prize went to Wallace Stegner for *Remembering Laughter*. The Atlantic Monthly Press books also shared in the anniversary. Walter Lippmann joined the list with *The Good Society*, and Clifford Dowdey's *Bugles Blow No More* was enduringly popular.

The main event of the year was the dinner celebration held on March 31, 1937, at the Copley Plaza Hotel, attended by more than two hundred authors, agents, booksellers, publishers, and friends, each of whom had a special affection for Little, Brown and admiration for its hundred years of success. We can do no better in capturing the feelings of that evening than by quoting some of E. Phillips Oppenheim's remarks from his autobiography, *The Pool of Memory*:

> I received a card of invitation to a dinner in Boston which was to be the source of so much joy and satisfaction to me. . . . Alfred McIntyre told me of the plans for this dinner and begged me to come. . . . Alfred pointed out that Little, Brown and Company had been publishing my books for thirty-four years and had just issued my 101st novel, and I had promised to come if I possibly could. . . .
>
> My dress suit, for which I had cabled, had arrived from London in time, and in a secret pocket I had the notes for my speech. . . . In an hour or so I should be on my feet trying to interest the crowd of men and women in my own personal connection with the proceedings, and never before had it seemed so insignificant. What right had I there by the side of the chairman anyway? More than a hundred books . . . Why, most of the people there seemed quite capable of having written a thousand. . . . Then a little voice of memory whispered to me, "Yes, but not so many published by the same firm."
>
> I felt reassured. It was an achievement, that. A remarkable feat of endurance on the part of the publishers or a triumph of pertinacity on the part of the author. . . .
>
> . . . With a throb of relief I realized that our toastmaster was approaching the end of his tether. He deliberately paused in his smooth gabble of reminiscence, glanced at his notes, and introduced the first speaker. And in a few minutes he was introducing me and asking me to be the guest to propose the health of Little, Brown and Company.
>
> I felt in my pocket for my notes and let them slip again through my fingers. I looked around the crowded room, and the faces of strangers seemed suddenly to become fa-

miliar. I felt that I was being greeted by friends, and the applause, which continued for some few moments, was a genuine expression of a genuine welcome. In those few moments I rebuilt my speech. I never once took my notes from my pocket. I let my thoughts wander back to the day of my first visit to the firm. I was shaking hands with Mr. James McIntyre, the father of the comparatively young man, seated by my side, who had achieved the proud position of being the head of one of the most distinguished publishing houses in America.

I was able to say a few of the pleasant things that I had always felt for the firm, and I was able to dilate upon the greatest pleasure one felt when working for a firm whose sympathies had always been so acute and vital. It is still a joy to me to feel — as I still feel and felt that night — that it is a wonderful connection to have, the connection between an author and a publisher with whom there has never been a single word of disagreement.

Well, my speech came to an end.

I felt, as I sat down, that it was the happiest moment of my life, and I felt, as I stood up again a few moments later, that it was also one of the thirstiest.

A New York publisher [Whitney Darrow], speaking for twenty or so others, was handing Alfred a silver bowl as large as a baby's cradle and the wine waiter was emptying champagne into it as fast as he could. Alfred was forced to take the first drink, but I had the second, and nothing ever tasted better. I wiped my lips with the beautifully embroidered napkin passed through the handle and finally resumed my seat a happy man.

12

The War and Its Changes

The centennial behind it, Little, Brown began its second century with a decade that soon was dominated by World War II. For publishing as an industry, the war had important consequences, but there were other forces at work in those years whose long-term effects would be even greater.

Little, Brown faced these challenges guided by excellent leaders. Alfred McIntyre was by now recognized as one of the most creative and astute publishers of his time. There were, in fact, those who felt that publishing was dominated by "the three Alfreds": Alfred Harcourt, Alfred Knopf, and Alfred McIntyre. Herbert Jenkins had retired as editor in chief in 1938, and his place was taken by C. Raymond Everitt. Everitt, who had been with Harcourt, Brace and Curtis Brown before joining Little, Brown in 1936, initially as New York editor, was politically more liberal than McIntyre and at times was irritated by the older man's middle-of-the-road approach. Still, they made a formidable working combination, and the trade lists they fashioned together contained many books of lasting value that sold very well.

This was essential, since trade publishing dominated the company's business. By 1938 neither law publications nor schoolbooks were performing up to budget, and the small medical department formed in that year grew only slowly and did not survive for long. The wartime rationing of paper finished it off in 1943 and the struggling schoolbook department a year later. McIntyre could not abide the thought that he might have to forgo reprinting a best-seller because the paper had been used by nonproductive departments.

"We thrive on best-sellers," McIntyre commented, "and languish without them." It was not just the sales of the Little, Brown editions that were important; equally significant now was the subsidiary-rights income such books generated. All trade houses were becoming increasingly dependent upon this extra money. The largest sources were the book clubs; the Book-of-the-Month Club and the Literary Guild had grown dramatically, and adoption of a book as a main selection by either club could make a difference of well over a hundred thousand copies in the sales of a popular book. Then there were serializations and excerpts, condensed versions, translations and foreign rights for an American book, hardcover reprints, and, as the forties progressed, paperback reprints.

Under the guidance of first McIntyre and Everitt alone, and later, when Everitt became executive vice-president in 1943, with the help of new editor in chief Angus Cameron, the trade list blossomed. Relations with authors were so good that many remained with the firm year after year.

A case in point is John P. Marquand, whose *Late George Apley* was followed by a string of popular and successful novels in the same genre. *Wickford Point, H. M. Pulham, Esquire, So Little Time,* and *B.F.'s Daughter* were all published during this decade. A like success was enjoyed by A. J. Cronin. *The Citadel* remained a best-seller on the 1938 lists, ending up as number two for the year. Several more Cronin novels were published in the next few years, the most commercially successful being *The Keys of the Kingdom,* which appeared in 1941, sold more than a hundred thousand copies in the first month after publication, and was number one on its first appearance on the *New York Herald-Tribune* best-seller list. All told, including Book-of-the-Month Club distribution, the number of copies sold came to more than six hundred thousand, a figure no other Cronin novel attained. Still another favorite author was C. S. Forester, whose Hornblower series appeared steadily throughout the decade and beyond.

These successes were surpassed, however, by the historical novel *Captain from Castile,* which Little, Brown published in 1945 and which sold 214,000 copies in its first month. It could have sold many more, but production was hampered by the paper shortage. By 1947, the grand total of copies sold, including the Literary Guild edition, was 1,343,367.

Samuel Shellabarger, the author of the novel, came to Little, Brown as the direct result of the efforts of Alfred McIntyre. Once or twice a year McIntyre would go to

New York and visit some of the literary agents. Paul
Reynolds, one of those so honored, wrote:

> None of the other presidents of publishing houses ever
> deigned to come to our office. . . . Everyone at the office
> was flattered that McIntyre wanted to call upon us. Be-
> fore his arrival we all scurried around to find something
> at least halfway good to offer him. Shortly after we re-
> ceived Sam [Shellabarger]'s seventy-five pages, McIntyre
> turned up. I gave him the partial manuscript. . . . McIn-
> tyre accepted the Shellabarger and turned it over to his
> editor, Angus Cameron, one of the best editors in the
> country.[1]

Shellabarger had been a professor at Princeton University but had resigned in 1928 to devote himself to
scholarly writing. Unfortunately, his private fortune was
wiped out in the Depression and he had to turn to more
commercial uses of his talent. He produced routine
thrillers and love-adventure stories, but his heart was not
in this work. Eventually, having cast around for something more sympathetic, he came up with the idea of
a historical novel about Cortés and the conquest of
Mexico.

Angus Cameron suggested *Captain from Castile* as the
title for the novel, even though the hero did not come
from the province of Castile but rather from Aragon, and
the demands of the plot precluded any change. Shellabarger wanted *Captain from Aragon* because it was accurate; Cameron insisted on *Captain from Castile* because it
was catchier. The author was finally persuaded to accept
the alliterative title. Shellabarger received hundreds of
letters about the book, not one of which mentioned the
inaccuracy!

Little, Brown also had wanted its author to use a pen name, on the premise that a snappier, more American-sounding name would help sales. Shellabarger, scion of an old Ohio family and grandson of a congressman, dug in his heels. This time it was Little, Brown's turn to give in. Shellabarger went on to write *Prince of Foxes*, a romantic novel about Renaissance Italy, published by the firm with great success in 1947.

Romances ranging from the exotic to the light and amusing appeared with regularity. Rumer Godden published her novels with an Indian background, *Black Narcissus* and *The River*, in 1939 and 1946. British author Margery Sharp came up with a welcome distraction from the war with the entertaining *Cluny Brown* in 1944 and *Britannia Mews* in 1946. The successful playwright Dodie Smith's first novel, *I Capture the Castle*, was published by Atlantic–Little, Brown in 1948 and became a Literary Guild selection. And of course there was always the steadfast Atlantic author Mazo de la Roche, continuing the Jalna saga with *Whiteoak Heritage* in 1940.

Little, Brown had published good mysteries for years. Two distinguished new authors were added to the list — the Atlantic's Geoffrey Household, with his classic thriller *Rogue Male* in 1939, and New Zealander Ngaio Marsh, whose *Death at the Bar* (1940) led off more than forty years of detective stories about the suave and intelligent Roderick Alleyn. Other notables included Helen MacInnes, whose romantic suspense novels were to prove enduringly popular, and the two men who wrote under the name of Ellery Queen.

Frederick Dannay and Manfred B. Lee were cousins who had started their careers as, respectively, art director of a New York advertising agency and publicity writer for the movies. As a lark, they jointly entered a contest for mystery writers and won, thus beginning one of the most successful collaborations in twentieth-century American mystery writing. For many years elaborate precautions were taken to conceal the identity of "Queen"; a masked figure would appear at autographing parties. Over time, Ellery Queen as both editor and author became one of the best-known names in the field.

Humor and satire began to figure more largely on the firm's list. The lighthearted verse of Ogden Nash advanced the cause of amusement with outrageous rhymes and unorthodox meters in such volumes as *I'm a Stranger Here Myself* and *Good Intentions*. Joining the firm's authors in 1942 was Evelyn Waugh with *Put Out More Flags*. Waugh's first four books, biting satires on the "beautiful people" of Britain between the wars, had been published in the United States by Farrar and Rinehart. None had done very well here, but Alfred McIntyre liked Waugh's work and had great faith in him. "It took tenacity," Edward Weeks remarked later, "to make readers believe that this man Waugh was far better than the American public then realized."[2] The tenacity paid off; Little, Brown not only began to publish Waugh's books but ultimately republished the Farrar and Rinehart four. Among the most celebrated was *Brideshead Revisited* in 1945, far and away his most popular book and one that has a whole new generation of admirers thanks to the outstanding public television series.

Waugh's early satires have a sharp edge, and his later ones are steeped in disillusion, but they pale beside the brutal misanthropy of Louis-Ferdinand Céline. In 1937

Little, Brown followed the publication of *Journey to the End of the Night* with the even more invective-ridden *Death on the Installment Plan*. The publisher approached the powerful novel with enthusiasm but also with some caution; booksellers were advised to "buy this book on the basis of [their] experiences with *Journey to the End of the Night*. A store that found that book completely outside of its scope should not attempt to force this on its clientele."

Of course the lists of these years were not entirely devoted to fiction. There were histories — *The Heritage of America* by Henry Steele Commager and Allan Nevins; and *The Age of Jackson* by Arthur Schlesinger, Jr., and *Scientists Against Time* by Atlantic author James Phinney Baxter III, each of which won a Pulitzer Prize. There were biographies — Samuel Eliot Morison's classic story of Columbus, *Admiral of the Ocean Sea*, another Pulitzer Prize–winner, appeared in 1942, and Dumas Malone's first volume of his definitive six-volume life of Thomas Jefferson appeared in 1948. Other notable books of the period included *Mythology* by Edith Hamilton, which has become the standard work on Greek, Roman, and Norse myth; Jacques Barzun's *Of Human Freedom* and *Romanticism and the Modern Ego*; and *Expectant Motherhood* by Nicholas J. Eastman, head of obstetrics at Johns Hopkins Medical School. This book has turned out to be one of the company's most enduring titles, still in print more than forty-five years after its original appearance in 1940, and used over the years by millions of women, and men, too, to answer their questions about pregnancy.

Many of the books published were concerned with the war. They ranged from Mollie Panter-Downes's *Letters from England*, an extraordinary account of the first year of

Samuel Shellabarger

Ogden Nash

Evelyn Waugh

Samuel Eliot Morison

the blitz, through many studies, novels, and tales of personal experience, including a collection of Winston Churchill's war speeches. One of the most imposing works to come out of the war was Samuel Eliot Morison's *History of United States Naval Operations in World War II.*

Morison had been commissioned in the Naval Reserve early in 1942 for the sole purpose of preparing this complete history, and he spent more than half the war at sea, seeing active duty on eleven ships and emerging with seven battle stars on his ribbons. He or one of the three officers on his staff personally covered every naval operation from 1942 on, and the books told the entire story of U.S. naval combat in World War II. The first volume was published by Atlantic–Little, Brown in 1947; the fifteenth and last in 1960.

Another Atlantic–Little, Brown book prompted by the war and the confusion into which it had cast the world was *U.S. Foreign Policy: Shield of the Republic* by Walter Lippmann. An extremely popular book, its career exemplifies what was happening in book publishing during the forties. *Foreign Policy* (1943), a Book-of-the-Month Club selection, was condensed in *Reader's Digest,* pictorially dramatized in *Ladies' Home Journal,* and syndicated nationally in newspapers. Next, it was republished in paperback by Pocket Books (a subsidiary of Simon & Schuster) and selected as an "Imperative" by the National Council of Books in Wartime. It appeared in book form in England, with selections in British newspapers and magazines, and was translated into French, Swedish, Portuguese, and Spanish. All told, nearly eight hundred thousand copies of all its editions were sold and distributed.

The war, of course, brought various hardships to the publishing community. Paper rationing was a major constraint, although the U.S. curtailment never got as low as it did in England, where by 1943 paper consumption had been cut by 62.5 percent. Military requirements and governmental directives affecting the transport and shipping industries caused backlogs at printers and binders. And there were manpower problems, hitting hard those firms that produced civilian goods. Various members of the Little, Brown staff left to serve in the armed forces, including Ross Whistler, the company's treasurer.

On the other hand, as Alfred McIntyre pointed out in his annual report for 1943, "The war has made millions of new readers of books and much larger markets should be available to book publishers without cutthroat competition if government, management and labor cooperate to a reasonable degree." This pious hope was not entirely fulfilled.

After the war, costs in book publishing began to rise steeply. All price controls were lifted, including those on paper and on wages. The cost of living soared, so that as staffs, depleted during the war, increased, so did salaries. Overhead costs rose sharply; Little, Brown now paid almost twice the 1941 rate to have a book typeset, printed, and bound. Paper prices went up by 60 percent; the cost of cloth had doubled.

McIntyre was worried about the prices for books increasing to a prohibitive extent, and he admonished his staff to maintain volume, avoid small printings, and keep to the minimum the number of unprofitable books. It also disturbed him that the chances of publication for promising young writers were lessening, since the break-even point for most trade books, which used to be two thousand to four thousand copies, was now between five thousand and eight thousand. His worry found words in his article "The Crisis in Book Publishing" for the *Atlantic Monthly* of October 1947. There he exhorted authors to take lower royalties until the break-even points were reached and manufacturers to hold the line on prices. None of this went over too well with the parties involved, and book prices still rose. Nevertheless, the public continued to buy, becoming used to the fact that everything cost more than it had before the war.

Still, even an accepting public was not loath to save a dollar or two, and consequently, during the war, paperback and reprint publishing houses began to do a flourishing business. Soon there were signs that a struggle for control of these houses would ensue. After Marshall Field, Inc., bought a controlling interest in Simon & Schuster and Pocket Books, the leading paperback company, it decided in 1944 to acquire Grosset & Dunlap, which dominated the hardcover reprint market. This move set off alarms at Grosset & Dunlap as well as in the industry as a whole. A consortium consisting of Harper and Brothers, Random House, and the Book-of-the-Month Club successfully bid $2,250,000 for Grosset & Dunlap. Shortly thereafter, Charles Scribner's Sons and Little, Brown were invited to participate in ownership. Said Bennett Cerf, chairman of Random House:

> . . . the story went that they [Marshall Field] were going to buy Grosset and Dunlap, which would give them the whole thing — the paperbacks, the hardbound reprints, which at the time were considerable, and original publishing. We thought it would give too much power to one publisher.

We hastily organized our group. We were the marines. We came along at the 23½ hour and we bought it, like that! The amusing part of it was that it had to be done fast, and there was a lot of money involved, and we all trusted each other because it was so big. If it had been small, we'd have sat there haggling for weeks. Mr. Scribner was the last man we called and he was the most cautious man in the world. He would argue over a two-cent stamp. But we told him if he wanted to come along, he'd have to move fast. He said, "Well if all of you are going into it, I guess it's good enough for me," and he went into it without looking at any of the figures.[3]

The speculation was that the five competitor publishers would never make a go of a common venture, but actually the arrangement lasted until 1967. Ironically, the hardbound reprints, which the consortium had so feared to see fall into the hands of Marshall Field, all but disappeared. The members, however, realized good profits from Grosset & Dunlap's other lines, especially children's books, and from the paperback line, Bantam Books, which had been started by Grosset & Dunlap and in which Little, Brown held a 10 percent interest. The arrangement finally ended when the partners decided to sell because their interests were no longer uniform.

The war also affected the management of both the Atlantic Monthly Press and Little, Brown. Ellery Sedgwick had stepped down in 1938 as editor of the *Atlantic Monthly*, and Edward Weeks was appointed in his place. Unfortunately, Weeks was away during much of the war period. In 1940 Sedgwick sold his stock in the Atlantic company to Richard E. Danielson, whose family continued to hold it until 1980. Chester Kerr came to head the Atlantic Monthly Press in 1941, and he negotiated the fifty-year contract between the press and Little, Brown in that year. Shortly thereafter he, too, went into wartime military service. Later he became a distinguished director of the Yale University Press.

The fortunes of the press and the magazine were closely linked. During the war, circulation of the magazine went up, but afterward major advertisers began to cut back on their budgets, and the firm was losing money. The Atlantic thereupon turned to Little, Brown for help, and the firm responded by buying all of a new preferred stock issue, a move that enabled the Atlantic to keep going. The return of Edward Weeks was an added advantage.

Little, Brown's own management remained essentially intact during the war. On May 23, 1947, however, the firm was shocked by the sudden death of C. Raymond Everitt, its executive vice-president. Only forty-five, Everitt was exceptionally able and had been groomed as the next head of house. Eighteen months later, in November 1948, came a second shock, caused by the death of Alfred McIntyre at the age of sixty-two. Faced with the need to find a new leader, the directors of the firm persuaded Arthur H. Thornhill, Sr., who was a vice-president of the company, to take on the role.

13

Postwar Expansion,
1949–1962

In the classic tradition of heads of house at Little,
Brown, Arthur Thornhill, Sr., began at the bottom of
the ladder in his career with the company. Charles Little, James Brown, and James McIntyre had all started as
apprentices without much formal education and made
their way to the top by dint of intelligence, initiative,
and sheer hard work. Young Thornhill was another in
the same line.

When he first came to Little, Brown in 1913, however,
Thornhill had no intention of remaining with the firm.
His father worked for the company as business manager,
and young Arthur came to help out at a moment of crisis
in the shipping room, on a strictly temporary basis. For
this work he was paid ten dollars a week, four more than
the regular stock boys received; they were not pleased.
They were even less pleased when it became evident that
the new colleague could complete his work in half the
time it took them. The manager of the shipping room
had also noticed the young man's energy and efficiency

and told Arthur that if he would stay, he would be kept on at the ten-dollar rate and promoted as quickly as possible. Arthur stayed, of course; one imagines that neither he nor the manager would have predicted that his career with Little, Brown would last for fifty-seven years and that he would end up as president and chairman of the board.

In personality Thornhill somewhat resembled James McIntyre. A quick learner, he was straightforward, gregarious, direct, persuasive, and candid. People accepted this directness because of his charm and his intelligence, and because he was usually right. Impeccably dressed, with a great sense of style, Thornhill knew how to deal with people. Perhaps his outstanding quality was his honesty. Thornhill liked to make a deal, but he always said that if it did not work to the advantage of both parties, it was not a good arrangement, and he always stuck to his word.

It seems obvious that this gifted young man would make a good salesman, and in 1921, when he was twenty-six, he was offered a chance to try selling. He was given a test: The sales manager instructed him to take a book that was considered "difficult" to the Old Corner Bookstore and see if he could sell a respectable number of copies. He succeeded, impressed the sales manager with his abilities, and was given a place in the sales department.

Soon people who knew him began to speak of Arthur Thornhill as a natural salesman. He would talk of selling as "painting a picture," and his pictures were so beguiling that he soon became a star salesman. In those days publishers' salesmen went on the road for extended periods, usually traveling by train and accompanied by huge display trunks. After arriving in a new city, they would set up the new books in a hotel display room, and buyers from the local stores would come to see what was on the list. Through this traveling, Thornhill came to know many people in the book business; his open, friendly manner made him easy to talk to, and he had a stock of lively stories he loved to tell.

Thornhill's next move, in 1935, after fourteen years on the road, was to the New York office, where he became senior salesman and manager. He was made a director of the company in 1939 and vice-president in 1940. As time went on, he relieved Alfred McIntyre of many duties, including the handling of subsidiary rights, and came to Boston for a week each month to work closely with the president.

When the board of directors chose him as the new president of Little, Brown in 1948, Arthur Thornhill at first was reluctant to take on so big a task, for he had suffered a serious heart attack in 1942 and was not sure his health was up to the demands of the new position. Fortunately, there were no problems. Thornhill got up early every morning, exercised moderately, and arrived at his office at 8:00 A.M. from his home in Duxbury. Luncheon was his time for communicating with others, at Locke-Ober, the Ritz-Carlton, or perhaps the Copley Plaza, where his guests might include favorite authors, of whom he had many; colleagues, especially young ones being encouraged on their way up; and buyers of subsidiary rights. Thornhill, who was a dynamo of energy, had kept his role as seller of subsidiary rights along with the general management of the company, and delighted in earning as much subsidiary-rights income for his authors and his company as he could.

Coming to Boston and assuming the position of so noted a figure as Alfred McIntyre was not easy, but Thornhill, with his years of experience as salesman, director, and vice-president, was intimately acquainted with the company's policies and operations. More important, he had the ability to step in and make situations work, as Millicent Bell points out in her biography of J. P. Marquand:

> When Alfred McIntyre died suddenly at the end of 1948 after seeing *Point of No Return* into print, Marquand lost the most prized of his readers. Under McIntyre's encouraging supervision he had made the transition from popular magazine stories to *Apley,* and McIntyre had helped him through each of his novels thereafter. In publishing circles ... there were immediately rumors that he would leave the firm — and solicitations. But Marquand refused these and later invitations to make a change and remained attached to the same house with a fidelity grown rare in modern author-publisher relations. The new president, Arthur Thornhill, became a friend without difficulty, although he was not an editor like McIntyre. . . . But Thornhill was also a man of considerable force and charm, with a robust, blunt practicality, good-natured and shrewd, who gave authors a strong sense of support. . . . Thornhill, who took no editorial role towards Marquand, offered him something else, a friendship more equal, fraternally sustaining.[1]

One of the strengths Arthur Thornhill brought to the company management was a new vision of the future. At the time he took over, trade sales were showing signs of a decline that would later become more pronounced, and Thornhill realized Little, Brown could not continue to rely exclusively on a relatively small list of law books and a trade operation dependent on best-sellers and strong subsidiary-rights sales. To compensate for the inevitable fluctuations, Little, Brown needed other sources of steady income. Thornhill moved to establish these with the founding of the Medical Division in 1952 (an earlier medical department had been dissolved in 1943) and the College Division in 1958, as well as the expansion of the Law Division in 1956.[2] This expansion required capital investment, and it is a tribute to Thornhill that he could set aside his own immediate financial interest for the good of the company. As the largest shareholder, he had the most to lose by new investment ventures, and, since these were financed out of earnings, he and the other shareholders collected fewer dividends.

Thornhill also sought to expand outside the company. In 1951 Little, Brown entered into an arrangement to publish and distribute the books of the New York firm Duell, Sloan and Pearce in the same way that it handled those of the Atlantic Monthly Press. The experiment lasted for only four years, since the editorial philosophy of the two houses proved incompatible. In 1954 Little, Brown (Canada) Limited was formed in Toronto. Since World War I Little, Brown has been represented in Canada by McClelland and Stewart Ltd; now the two firms joined to found the new company, with McClelland and Stewart holding 40 percent of the shares and managing the new venture. This lasted until the end of 1968, when Little, Brown bought the McClelland shares, but the operation remained under the able direction of Jack

McClelland until the end of 1985, when McClelland and
Stewart Ltd was sold to Avi Bennett. McClelland and
Stewart, considered to be the outstanding original pub-
lisher of Canadian literature, continues to operate the
day-to-day business of Little, Brown and Company
(Canada) Ltd.

Not all of the events of the 1950s were so happy. The
early part of that decade was sullied by the anti-Commu-
nist witch-hunting led by Senator Joseph McCarthy,
and in 1951 Little, Brown came under attack by the
McCarthy zealots who were persecuting so many loyal
citizens. Anyone who was in any way involved in even
mildly liberal politics was game for the McCarthy forces,
and Little, Brown's trade editor in chief, Angus Cameron, had long been a member of various reform move-
ments. In August 1951 *Counterattack,* a virulently reactionary periodical, denounced Cameron's influence at
Little, Brown, alleging that he was responsible for leading this "fine old firm" politically astray. Some equally
reactionary members of the national press took up the
attack in their journals.

As a result, extreme rightist groups turned their attention to Arthur Thornhill himself, harassing him with
telephone calls at his home at all hours. In an interview,
Thornhill stated: "We believe neither in prescribing nor
proscribing books. Books reflect and criticize life and in
so doing expose the conflicts, differences of opinion, convictions and beliefs of many men and women. . . . Under
this policy we have published thousands of books reflecting many points of view."[3] Many of the books being denounced were, in fact, not controversial, some were out
of print, some had not even been published by Little,

Brown, and others, as the firm pointed out in a four-page reply to the *Counterattack* charges, had not yet been written and could not possibly be judged without knowledge of their contents. There were, as there should be in a firm that does not confine itself to one narrow range of opinions, some books that could be called left of center. The attacks continued.

Then, in September, Angus Cameron recommended the publication of *Spartacus,* a portrait of the leader of the most successful slave revolt in ancient Rome written by Howard Fast, an author well known for his vivid historical novels, many of them sympathetic to radical causes, and himself an avowed Communist. The board, which at this time had no outside directors and which participated in the editorial decision-making process, disagreed. Not only did they turn down Fast's novel, they also voted that Cameron must obtain approval of his outside activities, as the directors themselves had done for years. Greatly upset by this attitude, Cameron submitted his resignation. It was an unfortunate episode. Cameron was a fine editor who went on to a distinguished career with Alfred A. Knopf, and the whole affair was deeply distressing to Arthur Thornhill, who had been Cameron's close friend and associate in both New York and Boston.

Nevertheless, Little, Brown and Atlantic–Little, Brown books continued to sell well, although as the 1950s advanced, fiction declined and nonfiction accounted for a greater share of the trade-publishing profits. Established writers of fiction did well, many of the two firms' loyal authors produced additional successful books, and some new names that in time would become very familiar appeared on the lists. These included H. E. Bates,

Lillian Hellman, Farley Mowat, and Peter De Vries. The
single Little, Brown novel that had the most impact,
however, was probably J. D. Salinger's *Catcher in the Rye.*
A classic of adolescent rebellion, this sensitive, ironic
portrait of a sixteen-year-old boy, highly critical of what
he sees as the hypocrisies of adult society, was published
in 1951 and has never been out of print since, having
been taken to heart by generations of teenagers. Salinger's subsequent *Franny and Zooey,* published in 1961,
was also a major success, and his short stories are well
known, but *The Catcher in the Rye* remains his undisputed
masterpiece.

A novel that rivaled Salinger's book in sales when it
was published and one whose title has become a catch-
word was Edwin O'Connor's *Last Hurrah* (Atlantic–
Little, Brown, 1956). O'Connor, the son of a Rhode
Island doctor, was one of the wittiest and most humorous
of men. Originally a writer for radio comedian Fred
Allen, he had devoted himself to work on his novel from
1953 to 1955, keeping his head above water by writing
television reviews for the *Boston Herald* at forty-five dollars per week. The paper fired him just before Christmas
of 1955, but by then O'Connor had entered *The Last
Hurrah* in the Atlantic Monthly Press fiction contest for
that year. The book was a clear winner and was scheduled for publication by the end of 1955, but Arthur
Thornhill, ever the salesman, suggested that it be held
until early 1956 so that he could personally promote it.
This he did to such effect that it became a Book-of-the-
Month Club Main Selection and was sold to *Reader's
Digest.*

O'Connor, although an Atlantic author, was personally very close to Thornhill and dropped in almost daily at Little, Brown for a chat, often followed by lunch. He had another success in 1960 with *The Edge of Sadness,* which won the Pulitzer Prize for fiction in 1962. Unfortunately, he died unexpectedly of a stroke in 1968 at the age of forty-nine, when, many felt, his best writing would have been still ahead of him.

Other well-known authors who joined the Little, Brown and Atlantic–Little, Brown fiction lists included Anthony Powell, whose *At Lady Molly's,* the fourth novel in his Dance to the Music of Time series, was published in 1958; Brian Moore, whose *Lonely Passion of Judith Hearne* won critical acclaim in 1956; Gore Vidal; Ved Mehta; and Mordecai Richler, whose *Apprenticeship of Duddy Kravitz* became a popular film. Richard Bissell's *7½ Cents* became both a musical and a film as *The Pajama Game. The Incredible Journey,* Sheila Burnford's heartwarming story of three animals' struggle to return to their home, appeared in 1961 and has remained in print ever since.

Notable nonfiction also appeared during the decade. As ever, history and biography were particularly strongly represented. In the spring of 1950 Little, Brown published *Captain Sam Grant,* the first part of a projected multivolume biography of Ulysses S. Grant by Lloyd Lewis. Sadly, the author died before publication, never knowing of the book's favorable reception and of course leaving the rest of the biography unfinished. Four years later his widow, Kathryn Lewis, met Bruce Catton, the winner of the 1954 Pulitzer Prize for history, at a reception and told him of her husband's uncompleted work. Catton was interested, but nothing more happened until

Mrs. Lewis got in touch with Arthur Thornhill, Jr., who took Catton to lunch and discovered that the historian definitely wanted to finish the Grant biography. Thornhill was delighted, but made it a condition that Catton obtain permission from Doubleday, his publisher, without which Little, Brown could not proceed. Catton did so, and *Grant Moves South* and *Grant Takes Command* were received with acclaim in 1960 and 1969, respectively. How much more circumspect was publishing behavior thirty years ago!

The Grant biography was by no means the only one on the list. Frank Freidel's four-volume life of Franklin D. Roosevelt began to appear in 1952, and *Proust*, a two-volume biography of the French novelist by George Painter, came out in 1959. The Atlantic's author Catherine Drinker Bowen delivered *John Adams and the American Revolution* in 1952.

More general nonfiction on the Little, Brown list included Homer Smith's *Man and His Gods*, the story of humankind's religions and their influence on thought through the ages, published in 1952, and *The Undiscovered Self* by psychologist C. G. Jung in 1958. Little, Brown also published a book in 1959 by a young writer who over the following years was to become increasingly important. His name was William Manchester, and his book was *A Rockefeller Family Portrait*. From Atlantic–Little, Brown came a runaway best-seller in 1956, *The Nun's Story* by Kathryn Hulme, and in 1959 James Thurber's *Years with Ross*, a memoir of the late editor of *The New Yorker*, sold more than sixty thousand copies upon its initial appearance. A notable anthology, *The Atlantic Book of British and American Poetry*, edited by Edith Sitwell, appeared in 1958.

John Bartlett's *Familiar Quotations* celebrated its hundredth birthday in 1955, an occasion marked by the publishing of the thirteenth, centenary edition, prepared by the Little, Brown staff. Since 1855 Bartlett's had earned its place as "a palace of pleasures as well as a court of appeals."[4] For those who wished to discover the source and the exact wording of "To be or not to be," "Cleanliness is next to godliness," "The only thing we have to fear is fear itself," and "Come up and see me sometime," the solution was still "Ask John Bartlett."

In 1948, when Alfred McIntyre was still president, Arthur H. Thornhill, Jr., came to work for Little, Brown. McIntyre had once told Arthur Thornhill, Sr., that he hoped both of their sons would join the house, and it was a great disappointment to McIntyre when his son showed no interest in publishing. Consequently he was delighted that the younger Thornhill was following in his father's footsteps. Arthur, Jr., had recently graduated magna cum laude from Princeton University, where his studies had been interrupted by almost four years of war service, first as an infantryman and then as a flying officer in the Army Air Force assigned to the Pacific. In spite of this he, like so many earlier Little, Brown executives, started at the bottom — in this case, at the Cambridge warehouse.

After some time, James Sherman, the company treasurer, brought the young man into the Boston office as his assistant. Next, Thornhill was sent to New York to gain some sales experience with both large and small accounts and later to work at the Scribner bookstore on Fifth Avenue. Reassignment to Boston followed; he worked in the trade sales department and got an in-depth look at inventory systems and costs, after which he

Arthur H. Thornhill, Sr.

Edwin O'Connor

The Board of Directors, December 1957
LEFT TO RIGHT: *Messrs. Robertson, Anderson, Williams, Gray,*
Sherman, Thornhill, Phillips, Emmons, Thornhill, Jr., Bradford

became assistant to Stanley Salmen, the executive vice-president and second in the company command. Here Thornhill performed a host of general administrative duties and learned the operations side of running the firm. When Angus Cameron left in 1951, Salmen served as editor in chief of the trade department for a short time, adding this to his other duties, until Howard Cady, Doubleday's West Coast editor, was appointed the new editor in chief. Cady, however, resigned shortly thereafter, and at almost the same time John Woodburn, the able editor in charge of the New York office who had brought J. D. Salinger and many other authors into the house, died. The company's executive editor, Larned G. "Ned" Bradford, who had joined Little, Brown in 1948, went to New York to run the editorial operation there, and in 1953 the younger Thornhill took charge of the Boston trade editorial department.

The search for a permanent editor in chief, however, continued, and in June 1954 resulted in the appointment of Nicholas Wreden. A charming White Russian, beloved by all who knew him, Wreden had come to the United States in 1920, worked in the Doubleday bookstore chain and then as a buyer for the Scribner bookshop, and finally ended up as editor in chief and a vice-president of E. P. Dutton. Unfortunately, Wreden died of pneumonia in August 1955, little more than a year after joining Little, Brown. Thereupon Ned Bradford was called back to Boston as trade editor in chief, a post in which he served with great distinction until 1969, when he gave up administrative duties and became a senior editor. J. Randall Williams, who had had a distinguished career with Macmillan, was appointed New York editor.

The year 1955 brought even more changes to the company. Stanley Salmen resigned, and Treasurer James Sherman took on the duties of general manager. At the same time Arthur Thornhill, Jr., who had become a director in 1953, was made a vice-president and general manager of the trade department. Under his direction, the departments of the company became more tightly organized, structured, and controlled. This was particularly true in the trade department, where more project meetings were held, more editorial scouting was undertaken, and closer cooperation between the Boston and New York editors was instituted. There was also more emphasis on the design of books. Little, Brown had always taken pride in the jackets, typography, and physical characteristics of its titles, but the time had come to reassess the handling of these aspects. On the sales front, direct-mail selling was further developed, and more emphasis was placed on the sale of foreign rights.

By 1960 the company had settled down after the major personnel and organizational changes of the 1950s. In June of that year Arthur Thornhill, Jr., was elected general manager and executive vice-president of Little, Brown, and a year later James Sherman retired and George A. Hall was appointed treasurer. Then in 1962, the year of Little, Brown's one hundred twenty-fifth anniversary, Arthur Thornhill, Sr., decided to step down as president and chief executive officer while continuing as chairman of the board. The board of directors thereupon elected Arthur Thornhill, Jr., to his father's former positions, and he moved into the front office to take over an increasingly demanding job.

Like the two McIntyres, the two Thornhills were very different people. In each case the father was a gregarious salesman, the son more private and introspective. All four men, however, had the same love of books and the same capacity for hard work, and all were equally effective in advancing the cause of Little, Brown.

Arthur Thornhill, Sr.'s term as president had been one of creative expansion, marked by one of the periods of greatest growth in the company's history. A risk-taker, Thornhill had looked into the future and realized that Little, Brown could not move ahead unless new forms of publishing were attempted. His legacy was the new Medical and College divisions and the renewed emphasis on law; the McIntyre days of relying solely on trade publishing were over. With this diversified base the company was well placed for steady growth in the future.

14

Medical Publishing

Although Little, Brown did not establish a formal medical department until 1938, the company had in fact published medical books since its founding. There were translations from the French, such as *Louis on Bloodletting and Louis on Phthisis*, and, probably as a consequence of Charles Little's interest in law books, Ray's *Medical Jurisprudence of Insanity* and Smith's *Hints for the Examination of Medical Witnesses*. The young Dr. Oliver Wendell Holmes was employed by Little, Brown in 1839 to edit and annotate a major British medical book, *Principles of the Theory and Practice of Medicine* by Marshall Hall, for publication in the United States. The subsequent success of the book brought Dr. Holmes considerable prestige.

For the next forty years the catalogues were sprinkled with medical titles, including several on military medicine prompted by the Civil War. The 1879 catalogue contained a special section on medical books, both British and American. At the turn of the century, however, with the emphatic swing to trade publishing, the firm allowed the medical books on the list to go out of print.

The small medical department that started in 1938 benefited from a distinguished board of advisers to help in the selection of books, but it did not perform as well as Alfred McIntyre and other executives had hoped. In 1943, during the time of the wartime paper shortage, the department was closed down and the list was sold. Some excellent titles were divided between Appleton-Century-Crofts and Williams and Wilkins, one of the most notable being *Gynecology* by Edmund Novak, which went on to become a staple of the Williams and Wilkins list.

Nearly a decade later, in the early 1950s, Executive Vice-President Stanley Salmen advocated the refounding of the medical department. He was encouraged by Dr. Nicholas J. Eastman, head of obstetrics at Johns Hopkins Medical School and author of the perennial trade success *Expectant Motherhood*. In an undated memo Salmen wrote:

> Dr. Eastman has urged me several times to persuade Little, Brown to resume medical publishing. He believes it is a wide-open field for a house with a good trade department which can assist in promotion and selling ideas. He says that our first start was bad because of staffing. He has offered to do anything short of running the department to help us. It was this enthusiasm that made me first think of medicine as one of the roots that could be put down to help weather whatever trade storms may be ahead of us.

Salmen solicited the advice of well-known medical authorities, including Baird Hastings, chairman of the department of physiology at Harvard, and Joseph Garland, editor of the *New England Journal of Medicine*. They were encouraging, pointing out that Boston as an outstanding medical center needed and would support a medical publisher. The most help came from Dr. Chester S. Keefer, chairman of the department of medicine at Boston University Medical School. Dr. Keefer became a close friend of Little, Brown's and advised on medical publications for many years, until the time of his death.

Homer Smith, a world-famous renal physiologist and Little, Brown trade author, told Salmen that medicine was growing rapidly. New hospitals were being built, new medical schools were being established, and doctors' incomes were increasing. Salmen saw a medical market that could only expand. "Despite its problems," he remarked, "medical publishing looks like a haven of calm compared to trade and we must seek what stability we can. Competition is serious, but not nearly as highly developed as trade. It is easy to forget, because we have the problems somewhat in hand, that trade publishing is one of the most preposterous activities in the economic world."

At this point Arthur Thornhill, Sr., asked Charles Woodard, the able head of the law department, to look into the possibility of reestablishing medical publishing and to prepare a report for the board of directors. On July 2, 1952, Woodard presented his findings. He believed that current conditions for medical publishing were unfavorable, that Little, Brown would be unable to compete effectively with the established firms, that it would take too long to develop a list. Medical books, he pointed out, were complicated, expensive to produce, difficult to market. Launching a medical department "would require substantial personnel and heavy capital outlay beyond our present capacity." According to his estimates, salaries for appropriate staffing alone would require a large capital outlay for the first five years, and he did not believe that sales would be sufficient to offset expenses. In short: "We should not, at the present time at least, originate a full-scale medical book program."

Woodard's report, however, did not deter Arthur Thornhill, Sr., who was fascinated by doctors and anything related to medicine, and in particular by the idea of medical publishing. His next step was to suggest a feasibility study, including specific suggestions as to what a medical department would publish. By a stroke of good fortune, an experienced medical publisher, Theodore Phillips, came to the attention of the board.

Ted Phillips, who had had a long and distinguished career in medical publishing at several Philadelphia and New York firms, at this time had no job and was eager to undertake the survey. He came up with a very favorable, somewhat overoptimistic report, and when the company decided to go ahead with the medical department, he was asked to head it. The new department began operating in the fall of 1952.

Before he joined Little, Brown, Phillips had been with the Blakiston Division of McGraw-Hill, which sold the list of J. and A. Churchill, a British medical publishing house, in the United States. McGraw-Hill had just decided to drop the Churchill list, and Phillips rightly saw this as an opportunity for Little, Brown. He arranged with his old friend John Rivers, the managing director of Churchill, for Little, Brown to become Churchill's sole distributor in North America.

This move had a twofold advantage: First, a ready-made list put the medical department immediately into business; second, the department had a chance to learn medical marketing techniques before acquiring its own books. The more than two hundred Churchill titles covered a broad range of medicine, and to market them the department was forced to develop a strong direct-sales program, work out effective distribution arrangements with the dozen medical wholesalers around the country, and initiate a plan for exhibiting and selling at national medical conventions.

Still another advantage of the arrangement with Churchill was that through it Little, Brown acquired the books Churchill published for the Ciba Foundation, a London-based independent organization that fostered international understanding in various medical fields by arranging scientific symposia. As a result of the symposia, about a dozen books on basic medical science, usually at the forefront of medical research, were published each year. Little, Brown sold large numbers of these titles to the Ciba Pharmaceutical Company in New Jersey (the supporter of the foundation), which in turn gave copies to researchers in basic science at medical schools and to libraries. This not only created goodwill for Ciba but also gained recognition of Little, Brown's new list by medical scientists, who were both book buyers and potential authors.

For a new medical publisher to win recognition is a slow and difficult process. Certainly the Ciba Foundation books helped; more important was Little, Brown's own name as a trade publisher. The company's literary tradition and high reputation gave the medical department staff credibility with customers and prospective authors that was extremely helpful.

At the start the department consisted of Ted Phillips and his secretary, with part-time help from the sales manager of the law department. Copyediting and production were handled by the trade department. The offices were at 34 Beacon Street in what is now the first-floor conference room. A few years later, in March 1956, Fred Belliveau joined Phillips as assistant manager. He had made extensive editorial associations in his former job at the medical division of Harper and Brothers, and was immediately helpful in developing the new Little, Brown list.

Phillips's efforts had already resulted in the acquisition of several sound, successful books, the most important of which was the very first one domestically produced by the department. A landmark work that has remained in print to this day, *Epilepsy and the Functional Anatomy of the Human Brain* by Wilder Penfield and Herbert Jasper came to Little, Brown through the good offices of George Hall, a member of the company's general administration. Hall's physician father was a friend of Wilder Penfield's and told the famous neurosurgeon about Little, Brown's entry into the medical field.

Another outstanding book, published just after Belliveau's arrival, was *The American Foundation Studies, Medical Research: A Midcentury Survey.* The result of fifteen years' labor, this two-volume work had a profound effect on medical research practices and focused attention on still-unsolved clinical problems.

In the same period Little, Brown published a book that was not only significant in itself but was also the foundation of one of the strengths of the medical department. This was *Principles and Art of Plastic Surgery* by Sir Harold Gillies and D. Ralph Millard, Jr., a two-volume set with twenty-four hundred illustrations, many of them in color. Considered iconoclastic, this book endeared Little, Brown to members of the just-emerging plastic surgery group and resulted over the years in the publication of many other works in this field, including *Plastic Surgery* by William C. Grabb and James W. Smith; Robert M. Goldwyn's *Unfavorable Result in Plastic Surgery, Plastic and Reconstructive Surgery of the Breast,* and *Long-Term Results in Plastic and Reconstructive Surgery; Plastic and Reconstructive Surgery of the Genital Area,* edited by Charles E. Horton; *Skin Flaps,* edited by William C. Grabb and M. Bert Myers; *Reconstructive Microsurgery* by Rollin K. Daniel and Julia K. Terzis; and a work of epic proportions, Ralph Millard's *Cleft Craft* — a large, beautifully produced work on cleft lip and palate, the first volume of which, published in 1976, won the American Association of Publishers' first R. R. Hawkins Award, an annual prize for the best professional or scholarly book.

In March 1959 Ted Phillips left Little, Brown to return to Philadelphia. At the age of thirty-two Fred Belliveau became manager of the medical department, and his assumption of control marked the beginning of its real growth. Belliveau traveled extensively to major medical institutions, searching out new authors and new book ideas, and many contracts were signed for future publications. Staff was still small, and Belliveau had a hand in all aspects of book procurement, production, and selling. The medical department still relied on the trade department to handle its copyediting and produc-

Theodore Phillips

Wilder Penfield

Fred Belliveau

Niels Buessem

tion. By the early sixties, however, the department had hired its own copyediting, design, and production staff, and a strong sales staff was soon to follow.

The medical department was fortunate to have its core management group form in the 1960s. Made up mostly of young people, this group provided a continuity that enabled the department to build a solid program with confidence and expertise. Judith M. Kennedy, who was to play an important role in the development of the medical department, started as a clerk-typist in 1961. She quickly made her way up the ladder, becoming secretary, advertising manager, and finally administrative manager of the department. In 1979 she moved into the general administration of the company and in 1981 became the firm's first woman vice-president. She was elected a director and the secretary of the company in 1983.

George McKinnon, the head of copyediting, joined Little, Brown in 1962, as did Clifton A. Gaskill, head of manufacturing. Lin Richter Paterson, who became editor in chief, started as an acquisitions editor in 1968 after working free-lance for the department for several years. Nancy Megley, who headed the journals department, started in 1966 and remained for more than fifteen years. As the department — now the Medical Division — grew, more space was necessary. In July 1964 the staff moved into the Thornhill Building at 41 Mount Vernon Street and remained there until 1977, when they moved to still larger quarters at 18 Tremont Street, their present location.

Planning has always been the theme for the development of the Medical Division. A program balanced among student texts, specialty monographs, and periodicals was envisioned, and the division selected youthful, flexible authors who had the potential to write more than one book. Books that were acquired early on and that have remained mainstays include Richard D. Judge and George D. Zuidema's *Methods of Clinical Examination;* Richard L. and Murray Sidman's *Neuroanatomy: A Programmed Text;* Max Samter's *Immunological Diseases;* Gerald L. Baum's *Textbook of Pulmonary Diseases;* Jacques Wallach's *Interpretation of Diagnostic Tests;* and Thomas H. Green, Jr.'s *Gynecology: Essentials of Clinical Practice.*

In 1961 the division had published its first paperbound textbook, *Pathology* by Thomas M. Peery and Frank N. Miller, which served as the model for a whole line of successful paperbound textbooks for medical students. The introduction of this series was a significant innovation and one later copied by other publishers.

Also in 1961 the division's first periodical was published, bringing a new and strong aspect to the list. *International Ophthalmology Clinics*, a quarterly hardcover publication, offered a clinical update of contemporary practices and procedures in treating eye diseases. The next year *International Anesthesiology Clinics*, a similarly patterned publication, was launched. In January 1965 Little, Brown produced its first softcover periodical. Fred Belliveau had negotiated an arrangement with the newly formed Society of Thoracic Surgeons and the Southern Thoracic Surgical Association for publication of *The Annals of Thoracic Surgery.* Several medical publishers had decided that these new societies were not strong enough to take on a journal. Little, Brown disagreed. The journal was an immediate success, justifying its publisher's faith in the societies and in its own ability to produce and market this kind of work.

Publication of one of the world's most prestigious journals started the next year. The *Lancet*, the oldest continuously published medical weekly in the world, had been founded in London in 1823. The first North American edition appeared in Boston on July 2, 1966. The content of the American edition was identical to that of the British, but the U.S. version was printed here with American advertising. A substantial effort was made to expand the American audience, and it could, of course, be delivered far more rapidly to its ever-widening audience on this side of the Atlantic. In 1973 Fred Belliveau and Arthur Thornhill, Jr., attended the *Lancet*'s one hundred fiftieth anniversary dinner at the Royal College of Physicians in London, at which Thornhill presented Paul Hodder-Williams, *Lancet* chairman, with the cover printing plate of the first American issue. It was a gala affair attended by prominent physicians and surgeons from all over the world. For more than twenty years, film of the British edition has been flown to Boston, and the issue has been printed here — an arrangement that has worked smoothly and profitably for all concerned.

A decade passed before the decision was made to expand the journal department further. In January 1977 Little, Brown first published *Annals of Neurology*, the new publication of the prestigious American Neurological Association. In 1978 came *Annals of Plastic Surgery*. This journal, wholly owned by Little, Brown, was originally a bimonthly but soon became a monthly as more and more authors wanted their articles to appear in it.

One of the division's most famous titles dates back to

the early days when future plans were first being made. In 1964 Little, Brown published the seventeenth edition of Washington University's *Manual of Medical Therapeutics*. For many years the house officers at Washington University's Barnes Hospital had written, printed, and sold the *Manual of Medical Therapeutics* through the department of medicine. Fred Belliveau during those years had visited Carl Moore, head of the department of medicine; eventually he persuaded Moore that the hospital should not divert its energies into the publishing business. Writing the *Manual* was one thing; manufacturing, shipping, and billing was another. Little, Brown took this cumbersome business off the hospital's hands, and sales of the *Manual* immediately quadrupled. Since 1964 a new edition has appeared every three years, each one outselling its predecessor, and Washington University's *Manual of Medical Therapeutics* is now the best-selling book in all of medicine, having sold well over a million copies in all its editions with the firm.

The success of the *Manual* led Belliveau to believe there was a place for other books of the same type: straightforward clinical material presented in a spiral binding. Thus was the Little, Brown SPIRAL® Manual series born. The second book, the *Manual of Surgical Therapeutics*, edited by Robert E. Condon and Lloyd M. Nyhus, was another outstanding success. It was followed by the *Manual of Pediatric Therapeutics*, edited by the Boston Children's Hospital; *Problem-Oriented Medical Diagnosis*, edited by H. Harold Friedman; and the *Manual of Dermatologic Therapeutics*, edited by Kenneth A. Arndt. These were later joined by Richard I. Shader's *Manual of Psychiatric Therapeutics*; the *Manual of Coronary Care* by Joseph S. Alpert and

Gary S. Francis; and James M. Rippe and Marie E. Csete's *Manual of Intensive Care Unit Medicine.*

Leading the way in establishing Little, Brown as *the* publisher of books dealing with the kidney was the ground-breaking *Diseases of the Kidney* by Maurice Strauss and Louis Welt, published in 1963. It was followed by Robert H. Heltinstall's *Pathology of the Kidney*, which has remained the authoritative volume in its field, and by Robert Schrier's *Renal and Electrolyte Disorders*; Chester M. Edelmann, Jr.'s *Pediatric Kidney Disease; Renal Function* and *Renal Dysfunction* by Heinz Valtin; *Clinical Nephrology* by Solomon Papper; and Milton Elkin's *Radiology of the Urinary Tract*, among others.

The publication of one book, *Human Sexual Response* by William H. Masters and Virginia E. Johnson, was enough to make 1966 a banner year for the Medical Division. Eleven years of research had gone into this pioneer volume. The authors, knowing their work was controversial because it had involved real men and women, and foreseeing the risk of sensationalism, wanted their book published by a medical publisher rather than a trade house. The Little, Brown Medical Division offered just what they needed. *Human Sexual Response* created even more excitement among scientists, the press, and the general public than had been anticipated. A book that meshed perfectly with the burgeoning sexual revolution of the mid-sixties, it became a best-seller. Masters and Johnson went on to publish other books with Little, Brown, including *Human Sexual Inadequacy* in 1970 and, with Robert C. Kolodny, *Textbook of Sexual Medicine* in 1979, but none was accorded the overwhelming reception given the first book.

By 1969 the time had come to give up the distribution
of the Churchill list, the importing and selling of which
took up time and energy the division believed could be
better devoted to its own titles. The division was prepared for a dip in sales following this relinquishment,
but nothing of the sort occurred. Little, Brown was becoming known and respected throughout the medical
community; the division's size and sales volume now
were approaching those of many medical publishers in
existence for a hundred years or more. In 1970 the division, with a staff of fifty people, published twenty-seven
books and four periodicals.

The next major venture for the division was nursing
publishing. Some of the earliest nursing books produced
by Little, Brown have remained best-sellers, including
Maternal-Newborn Nursing and *Child Health Nursing* by
Adele Pillitteri. Others were *Principles and Practice of Intra-
venous Therapy* by Ada L. Plumer and *Critical Care Nursing*
by Cornelia V. Kenner, Cathie E. Guzzetta, and Barbara
Dossey, which won an *American Journal of Nursing* Book of
the Year Award and brought Little, Brown much praise
for its sensitivity and depth of coverage. There were also
books important to the development of nursing as a profession, such as *The Advance of American Nursing* by Philip
A. Kalisch and Beatrice J. Kalisch; *Nursing Theory* by
Barbara J. Stevens; and the Nursing Development Conference Group's *Concept Formalization in Nursing*. It took
about ten years for the nursing titles to come of age, and
the nursing editors used the medical list as a springboard
just as the medical editors had relied on Little, Brown's
reputation in trade books. In 1983 the general management of the company decided that the nursing list should

be transferred to the College Division. The pattern of nursing education had been changing, with more and more nursing courses being taught at colleges, and it was felt that the College Division could market and promote these books more effectively.

Next, the Medical Division turned to the emerging specialty of allied health. The goal was not to publish a great many new titles immediately but to work them in slowly and selectively. Little, Brown in 1975 started a program of books in speech and hearing, laboratory technology, respiratory technology, and radiologic technology. Later came such works as *Basic Medical Microbiology* by Robert F. Boyd and Brian G. Hoerl; *Current Respiratory Care* by Kenneth F. MacDonnell and Maurice S. Segal; and one of the division's all-time best-sellers, *Emergency Care in the Streets* by Nancy L. Caroline.

Even with all this expansion into related fields, the core of the division lay in works dealing with medicine proper. Among the largest editorial undertakings in this subject were the anatomy books of Richard Snell, a prodigious author who, as Fred Belliveau remembers, originally showed up at Little, Brown without any fanfare:

> One day the receptionist phoned me saying that a Dr. Snell was here and would like to see me. In came a friendly British doctor carrying a good-sized briefcase. He told me how he had studied the catalogues of the various medical publishers and he found that we did not have any medical student texts in anatomy. We were just the sort of company he was looking for. He reached into his briefcase and pulled out a completed manuscript for a textbook of embryology for medical students. He asked if we would be interested in publishing it. I couldn't be-

lieve it. It usually takes years to locate anatomy professors who will write major texts and then additional years of waiting while they actually write them. Not only did he have his *Clinical Embryology for Medical Students* ready to turn over to us, but he casually asked if we would be interested in publishing a textbook of gross anatomy. . . . This became Snell's *Clinical Anatomy for Medical Students*, one of the best-selling texts in anatomy worldwide.

During the 1970s the international market for medical books boomed. English had become the lingua franca of medicine, and American medicine, with its acknowledged excellence, was very exportable. More books went abroad than ever before, and arrangements were made with agents throughout the world to stock Little, Brown books for their markets. The company also formed two joint venture companies, MEDSI Brazil and MEDSI Japan, to sell books more effectively in those countries.

With the Medical Division's maturity and stature, the time came in the early 1980s to compete in the toughest field of all — internal medicine. At this point there were two major textbooks on the market, the more recent having originally appeared thirty years earlier. In 1983 Jay H. Stein, chairman of the department of medicine at the University of Texas at San Antonio, took on the formidable task of organizing and writing *Internal Medicine*, with the assistance of nine section editors. Through a carefully thought-out and well-executed promotion campaign, Little, Brown sold more than its budgeted goal. Stein presented the subject of internal medicine in a contemporary fashion, matching the way it is actually taught today, and success rewarded his efforts. The author, his associates, and his publisher were so impressed by the reception given the first edition that they immediately began to make plans for the second.

In 1984 the Medical Division received its second R. R. Hawkins Award, this time for *Mastery of Surgery* by Lloyd Nyhus and Robert Baker. This 1,540-page, two-volume reference work, aimed at the practicing surgeon, showed how masters of surgical techniques performed specific operating procedures. It is a book that will continue on the list for years to come.

The year 1983 saw important changes within the division. Fred Belliveau let it be known that he had developed parkinsonism and had decided to retire at the end of June 1986. It was agreed that a new general manager of the division should be brought in at once to effect a smooth transition. Fortunately Niels C. Buessem, an experienced medical publisher who had been president of Grune and Stratton, had founded the medical division at John Wiley and Sons, and had been second in command at W. B. Saunders, was interested in coming to Boston and, after discussions with Arthur Thornhill, Jr., joined the firm in October 1983. Since then he has made several new appointments, including Lynne Herndon as editor in chief; Vincent Douglas as director of marketing; Howard Riley as sales manager; Carole Baker as managing editor; and Anne Orens as circulation manager. The newcomers are working successfully with such veterans as Joel Baron, Clifton Gaskill, Carol Rougvie, and Jim Krosschell.

By 1985 the Medical Division had almost five hundred titles in print and about seventy employees. It publishes approximately fifty books a year. The last fifteen years have seen the division's growth from a publisher of modest importance to one of the major medical publishing firms.

Fred Belliveau's approach to medical publishing was eclectic, sound, and practical, keeping a balance between texts and clinical works. Books on subjects in the forefront of medicine were chosen; those on fads were avoided. A fine reputation was gained by preparing books with taste, care, style, and aesthetics. Those who worked on the closely knit medical team all shared the same philosophy. Distinguished authors sought out Little, Brown as their publisher and returned to it again and again. In April 1986 the division acquired College-Hill Press, a San Diego–based company founded by Dr. Sadanand Singh and his late wife, Kala, in 1978. They were most successful in establishing a list of publications dealing with speech pathology, language, and special education. There are also significant plans for expanding the journal program. Certainly the future, based on thirty-four years of excellence, is promising. Arthur Thornhill, Sr., would have been proud of the division whose foundation he so enthusiastically championed.

15

The College Division

O nce the Medical Division was well under way, in the late 1950s, Arthur Thornhill, Sr., was convinced that the next move should be into the field of college text publishing. Young men and women were attending college in ever-increasing numbers, and the proposal met with more agreement on the part of the board of directors than had the prior one for entering medical publishing. There was concern about financing another new operation, but the board voted to go ahead.

The first requirement was a manager. Several Little, Brown executives who had had experience in the college field began the search. J. Randall Williams, New York editor, was acquainted with college publishing through his former position at Macmillan; Treasurer James Sherman had headed the school department at Little, Brown before the war; and Ned Bradford, trade editor in chief, had had college experience at Harcourt, Brace. Together the three men listed the names of many likely candidates.

A leading one was James B. Plate, then science editor at Prentice-Hall, who Bradford heard might be interested in the position. Plate was interviewed by members of the board, along with other candidates, and was their first unanimous choice. The College Division was founded in May 1958, with the thirty-four-year-old Plate as its head.

Plate rapidly set about building up a management team. He hired one of his former colleagues from Prentice-Hall, Donald R. Hammonds, as editor in chief and another Prentice-Hall associate, Milton H. Johnson, Jr., as western sales manager and editorial scout. Sales representatives in the college department were particularly important, for not only did they have the primary task of presenting appropriate texts to professors on the campuses, they also were responsible for gleaning information about potential new manuscripts. Johnson's territory was very large, and he must have been relieved to be able to split it with Warren B. Stone, who arrived in 1960 from Thomas Y. Crowell. Thereafter Johnson was based in San Francisco and covered the northern tier of western states; Stone, based in southern California, handled the Southwest. In 1961 Alfred L. Browne joined the department as eastern sales manager, and these five young men, eager to build the best college list in the shortest amount of time, remained with Little, Brown for many years.

James Plate had the goals for his department clearly in mind and knew how to delegate responsibility, giving his colleagues free rein in their methods for achieving results. Hammonds, who had been brought to the firm because of his editorial imagination, would point out possible directions, and Plate would narrow and focus them. One of the reasons for the department's success was the realization that books needed to be specifically designed for classroom use if they were to make their way onto supplementary reading lists, let alone be adopted for class use.

It would have been natural, given Plate's interest in and knowledge of science, for the fledgling division's first efforts to be in that field, but science books took a good deal of time to prepare, and Plate and Hammonds wanted to get into business quickly. Although a few excellent science books were published during the early days, emphasis was put on English and on political science.

The very first book on the college department's list was significant because its authors — Sylvan Barnet, Morton Berman, and William Burto, soon to be known as the "three B's" — were outstanding discoveries. Barnet, Berman, and Burto had been graduate students together at Harvard. After receiving their Ph.D.'s in the mid-1950s, they went out to teach literature — Barnet to Tufts University, Berman to Boston University, and Burto to the University of Lowell. The three decided to prepare a collection of essays about literature, with a glossary of literary terms, and submitted the project to a midwestern publisher in 1958. As a courtesy to Richard S. Beal, Berman's colleague at Boston University and a friend of Donald Hammonds's, they submitted it as well to the Little, Brown College Division, which at that time consisted of Plate, Hammonds, and a secretary.

Barnet telephoned the secretary to tell her that he and his associates had decided to sign a contract with the other publisher and that Little, Brown need do no more. An hour later Hammonds called Barnet back and exercised his by no means slim powers of persuasion. Minds were changed, a contract was signed, and a long and rewarding association of authors and publisher began. *The Study of Literature: A Handbook of Critical Essays and Terms* was published in 1960, and that same year the three B's also published *A Dictionary of Literary Terms.* In 1961 these were followed by the comprehensive *Introduction to Literature.* Now in its eighth edition, it has sold more than a million copies to students over the past twenty-five years. On the current Little, Brown list there are altogether nine books written by at least one of the three B's that have gone through two to eight editions.

Another book in the field of literature that has been significant in the history of the division is Randall E. Decker's *Patterns of Exposition,* first published in 1966 and now in its tenth edition. It is remarkable that a collection of expository essays, a literary form subject to constant changes in taste, has sold hundreds of thousands of copies and is still a leading seller on the list. There is hardly a teacher of college English who is not familiar with Decker's book, and it was a great help in establishing Little, Brown's reputation in the field of English.

Political science, the other realm Plate chose to enter, was an exciting area of study in the 1960s, when political scientists were coming to realize that they were working in the same fields as other social scientists; only the methodologies were different. Political scientists began to rely on systems and quantification rather than on narrative and descriptive analysis of history, bringing the two approaches closer together. Little, Brown embodied this new focus in the prestigious Series in Comparative Politics, which consists of two parts, Analytic Studies and Country Studies. Under the direction of two distinguished consulting editors, Gabriel A. Almond and Lucian W. Pye, the series has grown to include some thirteen titles.

At the same time the firm embarked upon publication of titles in the field of sociology. Such excellent books as *State and Society* by Reinhard Bendix, *Socialization and Society* by John A. Clausen, and S. N. Eisenstadt's *Comparative Perspectives on Social Change* joined the list. These, along with the political science titles, were creative ventures to meet the needs of an expanding and changing college curriculum, often creating a course by supplying the right titles for it. Yet they were all supplementary reading books, not basic texts.

A move into the market of core texts came in the 1970s. One of the earliest was *Writing Well* by Donald Hall. Hall, a poet and master of the language, taught English composition. Tired of poorly written, prosaic textbooks, he decided to write his own. Most books on writing give dictionary definitions for the parts of speech, such as "Verbs are words that express action, occurrence, or existence (a state of being)" or "[Verbs] belong to a large class of words that name actions or states of being and are inflected for number, person, tense, and mood." Compare Hall on verbs: "Verbs act. Verbs move. Verbs do. Verbs strike, soothe, grin, cry, exasperate, decline, fly, hurt and heal. Verbs make writing go, and they matter more to our language than any other part of speech." Needless to say, *Writing Well*, published in 1973, was an immediate hit and added luster to the expanding Little, Brown English list.

James B. Plate

Chester C. Lucido

THE COLLEGE DIVISION   145

Another core English text, published about the same
time, was by the three B's: *Types of Drama: Plays and
Essays*, published in 1972 and now in its fourth edition.
Little, Brown entered the science field in 1971 with the
publishing of a unique book, intended for the nonscience
majors who enroll in "Physics for Poets" courses. To
them Paul G. Hewitt offered a totally new approach in
his *Conceptual Physics*, which emphasizes understanding
of the concepts of physics rather than its specific mathematics and is written in a way that makes its subject
interesting, comprehensible, even exciting. A book that
concurrently expanded the market for physics texts themselves, *Conceptual Physics* ranks as one of the College
Division's all-time best-sellers and is now in its fifth
edition.

To be sure, not all of the introductory core texts the
division published in the 1970s were successful. Many of
them were too advanced for average students and, although high-level critical successes, did not sell in large
numbers. Among those that did succeed were *Exploring
the Cosmos,* an astronomy text by Louis Berman and John
C. Evans, now in its fifth edition; and *World Trade and
Payments* by Richard E. Caves and Ronald W. Jones,
which is in its fourth edition. Another political science
book, Graham T. Allison's *Essence of Decision: Explaining
the Cuban Missile Crisis,* first published in 1971, continues
to sell well year after year because of the masterful fashion in which it offers a case study on decision making
under pressure.

The 1970s brought change in both location and management of the College Division as it expanded. From its
offices in the Thornhill Building at 41 Mount Vernon
Street it moved to rented quarters at 11 Beacon Street, a

building in which several Little, Brown departments and divisions were housed during that decade. In 1968 Jim Plate was asked to move into the general administration of the company, where he was in charge of administering the three divisions involved with higher education: college, medicine, and law. Donald Hammonds became the general manager of the College Division, remaining in this position until 1973, when he left for Addison-Wesley Publishing Company, where he is now president and chief executive officer. From 1973 until 1977 S. Woodworth Chittick, a young M.B.A. who had served as business manager of the division, took over as general manager. In 1977 Chester C. Lucido, Jr., began a period of strong management that continues today. Lucido had been the publisher of Glencoe Press, an imprint of Macmillan's in southern California, and before that had served in various marketing and editorial posts at Prentice-Hall. He combined the duties of editor in chief with those of general manager for two years and focused the division's efforts on basic textbooks. In 1979 Garret J. White was employed as the new editor in chief. Lucido and White had worked together at Prentice-Hall and were in agreement on the division's strategy for the 1980s. In that year the division moved again, this time to 18 Tremont Street.

Earlier during this period of change it was agreed that a special department should be formed within the division to publish books for the junior college market, which several people felt had its own, idiosyncratic needs that were not met by college publishers. Founded in 1973, this department, known as Educational Associates, was headed by Alfred Browne, who had been serving as director of marketing for the division. Alas, it was not a success. Educational Associates tried so many different kinds of publishing that it was difficult to coordinate the various activities. It published some straightforward junior college texts; worked with Time Inc. — Little, Brown's corporate parent since 1968 — on collaborative efforts; prepared works for the vocational-technical market; produced educational materials tied in with courses offered on television; and attempted facsimile publishing. The plate was too full, and after three years the management decided to close the department and transfer the books Educational Associates had published into the College Division.

There was one book that made the entire Educational Associates experiment worthwhile. This was *Photography* by Barbara London Upton and John Upton, published a month after Educational Associates' official demise. The two authors had arranged through Educational Associates to adapt material from Time Inc.'s Life Library of Photography series into a book that could be used as a college text. John Upton was a well-known teacher of photography and Barbara London Upton, who had been working for a filmstrip producer, had vast experience in describing a concept within a prescribed space — precisely the kind of background needed for *Photography*. The book is designed in such a way that each double-page spread contains all the material needed for a particular topic, and this artful fit of captions, pictures, and text made the book easy to use. Now in its third edition, *Photography* has dominated the field and remains one of the most successful books on the Little, Brown college list.

By the mid-1970s Lucido and White realized that to compete successfully in the student market with major texts, to gain a real share of the increasingly competitive basic-course market, textbooks would have to be "developed." That is, instead of a manuscript being published pretty much as the author had written it, with only modest revisions by both author and editor, books would have to be planned ahead through careful coordination between publisher and author from the start to the finish of the publication process. Not all books on the College Division list are extensively developed, but those that are often include instructor's manuals, test banks, and other resource materials to enable the professors who adopt them to teach their courses more effectively.

A perfect example of a developed book is H. Ramsay Fowler's *The Little, Brown Handbook,* a basic text in grammar and usage, prepared in collaboration with the editors of Little, Brown. The College Division contracted for the book in 1974, but it did not appear until 1980, since it proved to be a complicated, time-consuming job that took a great deal of in-house development, most of which was done by Developmental Editor Jane E. Aaron. With this book Little, Brown was aiming at a field that had previously proved difficult to enter. The English composition handbook market was dominated by two leading texts; other publishers who had tried to compete had brought out books that were essentially clones and that ended up with very modest success. *The Little, Brown Handbook* looked very different from its competitors, and there was immediate consensus that it was a better reference guide and classroom text. Serving it in good stead was the excellent reputation enjoyed by the

English books published by the College Division over the years. Professors expected Little, Brown to prepare a superior handbook and were not disappointed.

Since the mid-1970s the main emphasis of the College Division has been on the preparation of basic texts, and its efforts have borne fruit. Not only is *The Little, Brown Handbook* of prime importance, Robert L. Lineberry's *Government in America* is a leader in political science; *Sociology* by J. Ross Eshleman and Barbara G. Cashion is an excellent introductory text; and *Psychology* by Henry L. Roediger III, J. Philippe Rushton, Elizabeth Capaldi, and Scott G. Paris offers an expert blending of current research and basic principles. Berman and Evans's *Exploring the Cosmos* and Hewitt's *Conceptual Physics* continue to be huge successes in their fields, as does John M. Lannon's *Technical Writing*.

Many of the division's books have been recognized as leading, authoritative texts that have broken new ground. For example, Robert J. Gordon's *Macroeconomics*, first published in 1978, combines theory and case studies in an exciting and relevant way. With it Gordon completely altered the teaching of undergraduate courses in macroeconomics. Little, Brown was the first to publish an economic update newsletter that discusses current economic trends and events and is supplied to professors who adopt *Macroeconomics*.

Recently, in the later 1970s and early 1980s, attention has been directed toward the improvement of student writing in all courses, not just those in the English departments. Good, clear, comprehensible writing is, after all, a basic requirement, regardless of one's major. Responding to this need, Little, Brown published in 1982

Writing and Reading Across the Curriculum by Laurence Behrens and Leonard J. Rosen, a book that met with great success and appeared in a second edition published in 1985. In 1983 another visionary text by the three B's attested to Barnet, Berman, and Burto's remarkable record. This was *Literature for Composition: Essays, Fiction, Poetry and Drama.*

In a completely different field, William H. Masters and Virginia E. Johnson turned their attention to college students with *Human Sexuality*, written in collaboration with their colleague Robert C. Kolodny and published in 1982. These enduring Medical Division authors found it quite natural to enter the textbook field, and the book is now in a successful second edition.

Two acquisitions enlarged the division in the early 1980s. The first was the purchase of Winthrop Publishers, Inc., from Prentice-Hall in 1981. Winthrop was a small publisher located in Cambridge that specialized in English, political science, and computer science. Its English and political science titles strongly complemented Little, Brown's own well-established ones. It was soon apparent, however, that the Winthrop computer science titles were, if anything, even more desirable, for computer science was a growth field that Little, Brown wished to enter. Three of Winthrop's core texts in this area proved especially valuable; they are Robert C. Nickerson's *Fundamentals of FORTRAN 77 Programming,* now in its third edition; *Fundamentals of Programming in BASIC*, now in its second; and *Fundamentals of Structured COBOL*, also in a second edition.

The other acquisition was an internal one, the transfer of the nursing text list from the Medical Division. In the mid-1970s the market for nursing texts began to change as more and more nursing programs were located on college campuses. The College Division had, starting in 1977, sold selected nursing texts to colleges, with the result that by 1983 it seemed practical to move the list from the Medical Division to the College Division, where it could receive the editorial and marketing expertise of a college-oriented group and allow the Medical Division to focus on its primary student and professional areas.

This development gave the College Division another fine career-oriented list, blending well into its strategic plan to strengthen its position in science publishing while maintaining its efforts in the traditional strongholds of the humanities and the social sciences. Since 1984 the nursing list has increased its revenues and become a substantial part of the College Division.

Selling books in the division involves comprehensive and well-coordinated market effort, which is administered by Janet F. Carlson, director of marketing; she has overseen the division's growth in sales during the last fifteen years. The national sales manager, Basil G. Dandison, supervises the activities of the field staff and their regional managers — the largest such staff in the company. The Little, Brown college field staff is extremely well trained, and many of them have moved to in-house sales or editorial positions from their original posts. There has been a marked change in the makeup of the field staff since the early days of the division. In the 1970s the representatives were all male and unmarried, and most were under the age of twenty-five; today more than half of the current representatives are women, about one-third are married, and most are older than their predecessors.

The editorial production department consists of staff

groups who coordinate the entire production process from receipt of manuscript to bound book. Managing Editor David Giele, hired by Jim Plate in 1964, supervises these groups as they produce not only quality textbooks but also a vast number of complicated ancillaries, such as study guides, test banks, instructor's manuals, acetate transparencies, slides, and software.

The College Division editors are well aware of what is needed for the future growth of their subject areas and of the division as a whole. The first twenty-five years of the College Division have produced a solid, high-quality base; now the strategies are in place and the directions set for the future. Talented staff and a strong sense of organizational goals provide a firm foundation for such optimism, and the division looks to the future with excitement.

16

The Law Division

From the early days of Little, Brown, Charles Little's knowledge of and interest in law publishing had put the firm in a unique position. Little, Brown's law books were among the most important published in the United States, and the company was the outstanding law publisher. Throughout the nineteenth century the healthy sales of law books assured financial stability, and the firm never lost the ability to select authors who were leaders in their fields and whose interpretations frequently shaped the law itself.

Often cited as the ideal model for legal authors is the preface of John Chipman Gray's *The Rule against Perpetuities,* published in 1886:

> I have long thought that in the present state of legal learning a chief need is for books on special topics, chosen with a view, not to their utility as the subjects of convenient manuals, but to their place and importance in the general system of the law. When such books have been written, it will then, for the first time, become possi-

ble to treat fully the great departments of the law, or even to construct a *corpus juris.*

Such a book should deal with the whole of its subject, its history, its relation to other parts of the law, its present condition, the general principles which have been evolved and the errors which have been eliminated in its development, and the defects which still mar its logical symmetry, or, what is of vastly greater moment, lessen its value as a guide to conduct.

This was the standard Little, Brown attempted to follow for all its law books, and probably none exemplified it more exactly than John Henry Wigmore's *Evidence,* published in 1904. Wigmore, a twentieth-century legal pioneer, took as his subject the field of evidence, originally explored comprehensively by his predecessor Simon Greenleaf in 1842 and by Wigmore's time one of vast complexity. No other legal authority has covered this topic in such detail. With prodigious zeal Wigmore researched, studied, and organized the subject into a scheme that has stood the test of time. To him the legal profession owes a tremendous debt.

A professor of law at Northwestern University, Wigmore was a colorful personality with strong ideas on many subjects. Among them was his staunch faith in scientific reasoning as the solution to all problems, a philosophy especially prevalent during the early part of the twentieth century. In *The Science of Judicial Proof,* which Little, Brown published in 1937, he attempted to develop "scientific methods of proof and evidentiary probability." Meanwhile, he was able to see *Evidence* through three editions — the second appearing in 1923 and the third in 1940 — before his death in 1943. Revisions of the great work have appeared over the years since then, and the book has been markedly influential in the movement toward the legal codification of evidence.

After Wigmore's book first appeared, law publishing at Little, Brown entered upon a rather quiet period that lasted until the late 1930s. Three factors seem to explain this development.

First, a school of thought called legal realism, primarily associated with Yale, developed around the time of World War I. The realists took the irreverent view (among others) that laws could not easily be codified. They believed that

> judicial decisions were not the result of a purely logical process nor were they value-free. Instead, judges made, rather than found, law; and in making law they were significantly affected by their socio-economic status. . . . Coupled with this skepticism, possibly cynicism, concerning the logical or doctrinal element of the law was the realists' conviction that since law was purposive rather than self-contained, law and law study seek aid from the related social sciences and should investigate the law in action rather than be content with a vision of the law in books.[1]

Thus there was much less interest in treatise writing during this period.

The second reason had to do with a change of emphasis in the legal publishing industry. There are two types of law publishing, primary and secondary. Primary source publication essentially involves printing cases and statutes as they appear. Secondary publications are works such as treatises in the production of which the publisher plays an active role. During the later 1880s, new legal publishers, such as West and Lawyers Cooperative, were formed and specialized in primary publication. The ebb in the writing of treatises, the form on which Little, Brown had focused, and the increased market for the primary source publications meant that the firm was not really oriented toward this new type of competition.

The third factor is probably the most important one and is to be found within the company itself. When Little, Brown purchased Roberts Brothers in 1898, it suddenly became a major trade publisher. Under James and then Alfred McIntyre, it devoted the majority of its efforts to trade publications. It is no wonder, therefore, that law publishing took on a secondary role and stayed in that position for nearly half a century.

Then, for reasons that are not entirely clear, interest in law book publishing began to revive at Little, Brown during the 1930s. Partly this may have occurred because of a renewed interest in treatises, and some of the most durable titles on the firm's list appeared during this decade. Partly, too, the resurgence of the law department may be attributed to Charles Woodard, a dynamic young lawyer who came to the company in 1939 and gave the department a needed stimulus. Woodard, briefly away in military service during the war, stayed with the company until 1954. Little, Brown was sorry to lose him, for by that time he had done much to move the law department forward, but he could not reject a handsome offer to be general counsel for the Gillette Company.

Also in the 1930s the department acquired an editorial advisory board to assist in formulating editorial policies and developing book projects. Until the 1950s the board consisted of a few Harvard professors, and its activities were very informal. The affiliation with Harvard was a logical one, since Little, Brown and the Harvard Law School had been closely associated for many years. The board was not without effect, and gradually a broader editorial program was developed. By the 1950s a larger board was established, made up of members of the law school faculties at Harvard, Yale, Stanford, Columbia, and the universities of Chicago, Pennsylvania, Michigan, and California. The editorial board was chaired by A. James Casner, then associate dean and Weld Professor of Law at Harvard. All the members were, and are now, prominent professors; some are authors, some are not. Today's editorial board members come from six law schools.

The new period of law publishing at Little, Brown began with publication of extraordinary works by Austin Wakeman Scott and by Dean Casner. Scott, a remarkable man who died in 1981 at the age of ninety-six, produced the first edition of *The Law of Trusts* (known now as *Scott on Trusts*) in 1939 in three volumes. The third edition appeared in 1967 in six volumes.

Casner is one of the leaders in the revival of the art of writing legal treatises. His book *The American Law of Property* was originally scheduled for the late 1930s but because of delays owing to the war, this eight-volume set did not come off press until 1952. Many of those who contributed to it went on to stellar careers in law schools and leading law firms. Casner's other major work, *Estate Planning,* was first published in 1953 and became one of the most important titles on Little, Brown's list. It started as a book for students and practicing lawyers; now it is an eight-volume reference set. Casner is a towering figure in the legal field; not only was he an outstanding teacher of property law in the United States, but also he can be considered the father of estate planning. Having literally invented the course in this field, he remains preeminent. For years Casner, a man of enormous energy, would spend full days teaching law at Harvard, then practice several days a week in Boston.

Two treatises published during World War II stand out: W. Barton Leach's *Handbook of Massachusetts Evidence,* which originally appeared in 1940 and is now in its fifth edition, revised by Justice Paul J. Liacos; and Charles Cheney Hyde's *International Law,* published in 1945, which was the first major work in this area. Leach, along with Casner, exerted a strong influence on the law department as an adviser.

In the 1950s, in addition to Casner's work, two other important treatises were published. The first was *The Law of Torts* by Fowler V. Harper and James Fleming, Jr., in three volumes. The classic work on the subject, it is now appearing in a second edition, with a third author, Oscar S. Gray, and in six volumes. The second treatise was by Louis Loss, who had been with the Securities and Exchange Commission and taught at Yale; his *Securities Regulation* appeared in 1951. This work, now in a second edition of six volumes, inspires enormous respect and is *the* book in the field.

The 1960s opened with another enduring work, James Farr and Augustus P. Loring's *Trustee's Handbook,* the sixth edition of a book first published in 1898. Grant Gilmore's *Security Interests in Personal Property* (two volumes), published in 1965, was a highlight of the decade. One of the best written of legal books, it won both the coveted Coif and the Ames awards. Born in Boston, Gilmore spent most of his academic career at Yale.

Four works published in the 1970s are remarkable contributions to legal literature. Phillip E. Areeda wrote, with Donald F. Turner, *Antitrust Law* in 1978. The work now appears in seven volumes and will be issued ultimately as twelve. One reviewer asserted that the authors are so preeminent that their work will be cited as law even when it is not and that it may thus become law. Other works are Tamar Frankel's *Regulation of Money Managers* (four volumes) and George E. Palmer's *Law of Restitution*, a four-volume title that represented the culmination of forty years of work. Both Palmer's work and a slim volume by Melvin Eisenberg entitled *The Structure of the Corporation* won Honorable Mention, Triennial Order of the Coif Award.

The 1980s led off with *The ABA Standards for Criminal Justice*, a four-volume work by the American Bar Association that offered a major blueprint for reform of the criminal justice system. Phillip McBride Johnson, former head of the Commodities Futures Trading Commission, wrote *Commodities Regulation*, published in 1982, the first work on that subject; and Wilbur L. Fugate prepared the revision of a classic work, *Foreign Commerce and the Antitrust Laws*, in two volumes. Other notable books of 1982 were Jeffrey A. Schoenblum's *Multistate and Multinational Estate Planning* and *Closely Held Corporations in Business and Estate Planning* by Edwin T. Hood, Sheldon F. Kurtz, and John D. Shors. In 1983 Peter Tillers published through Little, Brown a well-received modernization of volume I of

Wigmore on Evidence. Phillip I. Blumberg prepared the
first volume of a four-volume treatise, *The Law of Corporate Groups,* and Russell Osgood wrote *The Law of Pensions
and Profit Sharing.*

Publishing treatises for lawyers is only half of the Law
Division's activity. The other half involves publishing
books for students. It was in this area that Little, Brown
once again came up with a first. Before the Civil War, a
legal education consisted primarily of attending lectures
given by a professor. Thereafter, a student who wished to
become a lawyer had to apprentice himself to a practicing lawyer and learn the real fundamentals of the law in
that way. Harvard professor Christopher Columbus
Langdell realized that a collection of cases on a given
subject would make the teaching and learning of the law
more effective. Through such collections the student
would no longer need the experiences and perhaps the
prejudices of a practicing attorney; he could study the
cases on a particular topic and learn how to approach
legal problems and their solutions thereby.

The first casebook, Langdell's *Selected Cases on Contracts,*
was published by Little, Brown in 1871. Other casebooks
soon followed. Melville Bigelow's *Elements of Equity for the
Use of Students* appeared in 1879; Samuel Williston's *Cases
on Contracts* in 1894; and Austin Wakeman Scott's *Select
Cases and Other Materials on the Law of Trusts* in 1919.

The casebook method of teaching was considered revolutionary; it did, however, catch on and has become a
permanent part of legal education. Essentially un-
changed since the time of Langdell, casebook techniques
have paved the way for a basic mass legal pedagogy,
have permitted the American legal system to grow, and

John Henry Wigmore

Timothy C. Robinson

have introduced a greater systematization and unifor-
mity into the law itself. The method has since been
adapted to other disciplines, notably business, and it is to
Little, Brown's credit that the firm published the first
casebook more than a hundred years ago.

With the 1950s, thanks to Arthur H. Thornhill, Sr.'s
imaginative expansion of the company into areas other
than trade, the enlargement of the editorial law advisory
board, and a striking increase in the number of students
attending law school, the law department began a vigorous period of rejuvenated growth. The law school text
department was started, and a full-fledged program for
producing casebooks emerged. Titles from that decade
remain key words to this day. They include Casner and
Leach's *Cases and Text on Property,* published in 1951, and
Friedrich Kessler and Malcolm Pitman Sharp's *Contracts:
Cases and Materials,* which first appeared in 1953 and has
as contributors the major intellectual figures in mid-
twentieth-century contract law.

Trial Tactics and Methods by Harvard professor Robert
E. Keeton (now a federal judge), first published by Little, Brown in 1954, initiated a revolutionary program in
the teaching of trial practice to law students, one that
has since been copied by other law schools. Another
major path-breaking book of the 1950s was *Administrative
Law* by Louis L. Jaffe and Nathaniel L. Nathanson. Jaffe
was a preeminent scholar and teacher in this field, and
the book went on to four editions, the most recent in
1976. In 1954 four leading constitutional law scholars at
Harvard — Paul A. Freund, Arthur E. Sutherland,
Mark DeWolfe Howe, and Ernest Brown — published
the first edition of the seminal *Constitutional Law.*

Boris I. Bittker has been a leader in the field of taxation for thirty years. His original work, *Federal Income, Estate, and Gift Taxation,* has now, in its fifth edition, been divided into three separate components. Bittker and Lawrence M. Stone published *Federal Income Taxation* in 1980, and a sixth edition, with William Klein as third author, was published in 1984; *Estate and Gift Taxation* by Bittker and Elias Clark was also published in 1984; and *Federal Taxation of Business Organizations* by Richard L. Doernberg, Howard E. Abrams, Bittker, and Lawrence Stone will appear in 1987.

In the field of torts, one of the two leading textbooks is Charles O. Gregory and Harry Kalven's *Cases and Materials on Torts,* an outstanding treatment of the subject first published by Little, Brown in 1959. The third edition, published in 1977, added Richard A. Epstein as lead author.

After Charles Woodard left in 1954, lawyer Rodney T. Robertson, the assistant manager of the law department, became the general manager. During his administration, Little, Brown's growth in the field of student books was given a considerable impetus by the purchase of twenty-four casebooks from Prentice-Hall in 1958. This addition to the firm's own, increasing casebook list put the law department squarely into the position of a major publisher for the expanding student market. Some of those titles are still on the list after thirty years and remain top books in their fields.

Another book that, like Casner's *Estate Planning,* created a field of study was William J. Curran's *Law, Medicine, and Forensic Science,* first published in 1960. Paul G. Kauper, the renowned University of Michigan professor, had published the first edition of his *Constitutional*

Law with Prentice-Hall in 1954, but Little, Brown brought out the second edition in 1960. The fifth edition, which added Francis X. Beytagh as author, was published in 1980, following the death of Kauper.

For more than thirty years the best-selling student book in criminal law has been *Criminal Law and Its Processes* by Monrad G. Paulsen and Sanford H. Kadish, published in 1962. The authors' approach to the teaching of criminal law was creative and set the standard in the 1960s, 1970s, and even 1980s. The fourth edition, published in 1983, has an additional author, Stephen J. Schulhofer.

The list of outstanding texts continues. An exceptionally well-written one, Fleming James, Jr.'s *Civil Procedure,* was first published in 1965 and now has as coauthor Geoffrey C. Hazard. The treatise by Phillip Areeda has already been mentioned; his student book, *Antitrust Analysis,* appeared first in 1967.

A Little, Brown author who has gained universal recognition is Judge Richard A. Posner, author of *Economic Analysis of Law,* published in 1973. Posner created a philosophy of the law that says: "Legal scholars should analyze a law's purpose and impact in terms of economics rather than concentrating on legal issues." Posner has long been respected for his intellect and creativity. Justice William Brennan once said that he had met only two authentic geniuses in his lifetime; one was Justice William O. Douglas and the other was Richard Posner. " 'Judge Posner has fundamentally changed the way people look at legal problems,' according to Douglas Baird, a Chicago law professor and Little, Brown author. 'There are only two or three people in a generation like him.' "[2]

While Posner argued that legal rights and duties should be understood in terms of economics, other books reflected the strong civil rights movement: *Race, Racism and American Law* by Derrick Bell; *Child, Family and State* by Robert Mnookin; and *Sex Discrimination and the Law* by Barbara Babcock, Ann Freedman, Eleanor Norton, and Susan Ross.

Other ground-breaking texts were published by the Law Division in the 1980s, beginning with *Administrative Law and Regulatory Policy* by Stephen G. Breyer and Richard B. Stewart. Thomas A. Mauet's *Fundamentals of Trial Techniques* has become the top seller of any title published by the division, and Jesse Dukeminier and James E. Krier's *Property* is beginning to emerge as the major book in its field for the late 1980s and the 1990s. In 1982 Little, Brown published E. Allan Farnsworth's *Contracts,* a modern textbook that has become the leading source for understanding contract law; and John Price's *Contemporary Estate Planning,* a successful text with a practice orientation.

As with all books from the Law Division, the casebooks are quality productions. Their design is distinctive and handsome. The books are bound in red with black and gold stamping, and the interior design of each is given special attention. All aspects of law book production are handled with great personal care on the part of the staff.

Today's period of the Law Division history began with the arrival of Timothy G. Robinson in July 1971. As general manager, Robinson, who had pursued graduate study in the philosophy of the law, brought a new vigor to the division. When he came, the staff numbered twenty-one; today there are thirty-seven people working in the Law Division. They publish approximately sixty titles per year, including supplements, revised editions, and new titles. Of course, a six-volume work is counted as a single title, just as is a three-hundred-page handbook.

The Law Division has made plans for solid growth in both of its endeavors, treatises for practicing lawyers and books directed toward students. It is initiating new types of publications (such as newsletters and loose-leaf material) and diversification of media (for example, publishing a book both in printed form and on disks). The division seeks a synergy in the kinds of books and authors it attracts, looking for authors with a combination of talents who may write a treatise and then undertake a casebook.

Shifts in legal thinking are carefully observed, for these changes will determine the publishing plans of the future. The legal profession continues to adjust as society itself changes, and thus the law stays fresh and new. New topics needing more attention are rapidly emerging: alternative dispute resolution, computers and the law, product liability, international business, regulation of health care, environmental law, employment discrimination, human rights in the world community. All are among the issues that may be subjects for forthcoming law books.

Little, Brown's tradition in law book publishing is unique in the United States. A hundred and fifty years of publishing legal volumes of impeccable reputation is a record that no other firm can match, and the company continues that reputation, selecting books that have enduring qualities. That is the Law Division tradition, and the tradition lives on.

17

Children's Books,
1925 to the Present

Children's book publishing from the 1920s on was marked by several profound developments. One of the first and most important was that for many years the field was almost totally dominated by two groups of women, the editors of children's books and librarians. Both groups were firmly dedicated to a crusade for improvement of quality and serious recognition of juvenile literature. Convinced that what children read had a deep and lasting influence on their characters and their outlooks, these women fought hard for excellence. Editors could pick and choose to select the best, and they were aided by the librarians, who urged them to look for and develop special books for children, designed for their specific needs and interests, rather than simply suggest that an adult author "try" something for youngsters. Together the editors and the librarians formed a bond that persists today; there is no such relationship between adult-book editors and librarians.

The movement for quality found a strong advocate in Frederic G. Melcher, one of the founders of *Publishers*

Weekly. In 1922 Melcher established the Newbery Medal, to be awarded annually by the American Library Association to the book that had made the most distinguished contribution to American children's literature in the previous year. This notable award, named for John Newbery, an eighteenth-century British publisher who emphasized the importance of children's books, did much to promote children's books to a new level of recognition.

Public libraries created special reading areas for children and trained their staff to understand what children liked to read and to select the appropriate titles. Branch libraries were being developed, and larger and better-equipped school libraries were established. Major publishing houses that produced books for children as part of their regular trade lists started to hire bona fide children's book editors. The first to do so was Macmillan, which in 1919 created a separate children's book division, headed by Louise Seaman. In 1926 Little, Brown followed suit, appointing Lucille Gulliver, a writer and editor, to head a department for the exclusive preparation of children's books. During her time with the company she laid the foundation for a list balanced both in subject matter and in format and continued the long Little, Brown tradition of quality juvenile publishing.

By 1933, however, when Lucille Gulliver left the company, the Depression was in full swing, library budgets had been cut to the bone, and the discretionary income for such "nonessentials" as a separate children's department had largely dried up. Little, Brown continued to publish children's books, but they were reabsorbed into the general trade department.

Another significant development in this area of publishing was technology. During the 1920s production costs generally were rising and the design of children's books was limited by price considerations. By 1930 the new photo-offset printing process made possible the publishing of color illustrations at a reasonable cost. Illustrations became important from this time on. Now a book could be produced in which the pictures virtually told the story, so that after 1930 there was a spectacular growth in the number and variety of picture books. Illustrators received their due recognition when in 1938 Frederic Melcher established the Caldecott Medal, awarded annually to the most distinguished artist of an American picture book for children and named for Randolph Caldecott, the famous nineteenth-century British artist and illustrator. Publishers also recognized that author and illustrator were often equal partners in the creation of certain books and should share the royalties.

Still another development was a shift in theme and subject matter. For a while the strongly moralistic thematic tradition of the earlier years prevailed. Many of the older books Little, Brown had published throughout the years continued to appeal, including all of Louisa May Alcott's books. Gradually, however, the themes became less romantic and more modern. Consider, for example, the success of *Heroes of Civilization* by Joseph Cottler and Haym Jaffe, published in 1931. Real-life achievers — men and women notable in such fields as exploration, pure science, invention, biology, and medicine — were portrayed as models. The book sold well for more than forty years and was followed by a sequel in 1969.

Many books with science as their subject became popular in the 1930s with the upsurge in scientific achievements. Such stories also led to the popularity of career books and biographies; an enduringly popular series by Helen Dore Boylston published by Atlantic–Little, Brown began in 1936 with *Sue Barton, Student Nurse* and eventually included seven titles. The life of Louisa May Alcott, *Invincible Louisa* by Cornelia Meigs, was published in 1933, won the Newbery Medal in 1934, and has remained in print ever since.

There was more room, too, for the light of heart. In 1938 the delightful *Mr. Popper's Penguins* by Richard and Florence Atwater was published, winning a Newbery Honor Award the following year. This classic book was the only one its authors wrote, but its illustrator, Robert Lawson, went on to a long and productive relationship with Little, Brown.

Lawson, whose talents as writer and illustrator made him the only person so far to win both a Caldecott and a Newbery award, told how he became an author:

> After [I illustrated] *Mr. Popper's Penguins*, Little, Brown and Co. said that they would like me to do another book and asked that I suggest some subject that especially interested me. Then they said they would get an author to write the story and I could do the drawings. They also suggested that perhaps a story about some famous historical person and his, or her, pet might be a good idea to work on. So I considered all the famous historical characters I could think of. The only ones that had pets were Cardinal Richelieu and his kittens and Cleopatra and her asp. Neither of these seemed very appealing. Then for some unknown reason I thought of Ben Franklin and that messy-looking old fur cap of his. It always looked to me as though it must be inhabited by *something* and why not a mouse? So suddenly, Amos took form. The origin of

the name is simple. AMOS — A MOUSE. . . . I wrote an outline of what I thought the story might be and sent it off to Little, Brown. They immediately wrote back that while they thought the idea was spendid they could not possibly find any author who could write such a cock-eyed story and I would have to do it myself.[1]

The "cock-eyed story" became *Ben and Me* (1939). Lawson's emphasis on Franklin the man rather than Franklin the legend and his charming, detailed, and precise illustrations have enchanted several generations of children. His subsequent books, including *Mr. Revere and I*, another tale told by a famous man's pet, have given him a firm place in children's literature.

During the 1940s many notable children's works were published. The new technology for picture reproduction was seen at its best in the *Tenggren Mother Goose*, with 144 pages of poems and full-color pictures on every page by the matchless illustrator Gustaf Tenggren. Wilma Lord Perkins produced a child's version of the famous original in *The Fannie Farmer Junior Cookbook* (1942), and several adult authors turned quite successfully to juveniles. C. S. Forester's *Poo Poo and the Dragons* appeared in 1942, and Margery Sharp began her delightfully fanciful Miss Bianca series, about the adventures of a band of mice, with *The Rescuers* in 1959. The tradition continued with such stalwart adult authors as Allan Eckert, whose *Incident at Hawk's Hill* won a Newbery Honor in 1972, and Walter D. Edmonds, given a National Book Award for *Bert Breen's Barn* in 1975.

After World War II ended, the sales of children's books rose markedly, making so substantial a contribution to the company's revenues that Little, Brown decided in 1950 to reactivate the children's book department as a separate entity. For editor the firm chose Helen Jones.

Miss Jones (as she was always known) had come to Little, Brown as a clerk in 1926. It did not take her long to determine that books for children were her special interest. From clerk she moved to the promotion of educational books and then became assistant to James Sherman, at that time the manager of the schoolbook department. When the schoolbooks were sold in 1944, Miss Jones became advertising manager of the trade department in charge of promotion of children's books.

Opinionated, feisty, and charming, Miss Jones represented the best of the "second generation" of children's book editors — not those who founded the industry in the twenties, but those who were their immediate heirs and knew from firsthand experience how it all worked. Miss Jones recognized quality and knew her market. She demanded exactitude, follow-up, and attention to detail. Always completely involved in the production of her books, she had a keen sense of the importance of the artist's contribution and was usually present when her books went on press to ensure that the printing came out right, particularly if color printing was involved.

Miss Jones's editorship brought an increased diversity to the children's list during the 1950s: adventure stories, historical tales, animal fantasies, and more career series. One of the stalwarts of children's books was recruited by Miss Jones in 1954. This was Matt Christopher, who was asked by Miss Jones if he would write a sports book for young boys, a field she had found sadly neglected. Christopher's first book, *The Lucky Baseball Bat*, was an immediate success and was followed by a long list of similar titles. Most of Christopher's books have stayed in print, selling well year after year, and he is still making important contributions today.

Meanwhile, the Atlantic Monthly Press decided to follow Little, Brown's example and started its modern children's editorial program; Emilie W. McLeod was the first children's book editor. Up to this point the Atlantic–Little, Brown list included about fifteen Atlantic books a year; now, under Emilie McLeod's leadership, the list increased to more than forty. The program started with the publication of Oliver Butterworth's *Enormous Egg* in 1956 and soon acquired a group of consistently successful contributors. Scott Corbett began writing his stories for boys in the 1960s and is still active today; Sid Fleischman was responsible for the zany McBroom series and a host of other equally delightful books. Marc Brown, creator of Arthur, the lovable aardvark, was brought onto the list by Melanie Kroupa, Emilie McLeod's successor, and his books are still going strong. The charming Bear stories by David McPhail began to appear, and the Atlantic's author Miska Miles won a Newbery Honor Award in 1972 for *Annie and the Old One.*

At Little, Brown, the 1960s got under way with *Le Hibou et la Possiquette*, Francis Steegmuller's French version of Edward Lear's *Owl and the Pussycat.* Illustrated by Barbara Cooney, who was to be twice the recipient of a Caldecott Medal, this was a surprise best-seller as popular with adults as it was with children. Another book written and illustrated by a subsequent Caldecott winner appeared in 1961. This was *The Wing on a Flea* by Ed Emberley, the first in a long line of successful children's

Helen Jones

Melanie Kroupa and John Keller

books that continues to this day. The American Library Association chose *Flea* as one of its notable books, and the *New York Times* named it one of the best books of the year.

The 1960s saw another dramatic change in subject matter and theme as America was shaken out of its post-war complacency to face serious social problems that juvenile literature had heretofore barely touched. For all the trend away from romanticism in the earlier part of the century, children's books had still displayed an amazing innocence. Now, however, such issues as minority concerns, divorce, single-parent families, and changing sexual mores began to come to the fore.

At the same time profits in the juvenile field surged. The blossoming of children's paperbacks dramatically expanded the market, particularly for books directed at the "middle-age child" and the "young adult," the new name for the teenager. Even more important in immediate effect were federal funding programs that affected publishing as never before. In 1965 the Head Start Program, which concentrated on the educational and cultural needs of deprived children, was started, and that same year Congress passed the Elementary and Secondary Education Act, which made available a billion dollars for school libraries, textbooks, and other instructional materials. Such a large grant resulted in some indiscriminate publishing, but in general it made it possible for many fine new authors of children's books to launch successful careers. Unfortunately, the federal largesse did not last for long, and some of those programs have languished, but the impetus given children's book publishing has remained.

At the end of 1969 Helen Jones retired after more than

forty years with Little, Brown, and Ralph Woodward
was put in charge of the children's book department.
Woodward, primarily an administrator, appointed John
Keller, who had been managing library promotion for
the department, as editor and two years later editor in
chief. Keller stayed in that capacity for ten years, left the
company briefly in 1982, and returned as children's book
publisher in 1985. That men were now involved more
closely in children's book publishing illustrates yet another trend.

During the 1970s Little, Brown continued to publish
many successful books under this new leadership. The
very popular Brown Paper School series, printed on
brown-tinted paper and offering a casual approach to
learning, was introduced with *The I Hate Mathematics!
Book* by Marilyn Burns. Lois Duncan, who had begun
writing under the aegis of Helen Jones, became widely
known as the author of excellent young-adult suspense
novels, and Ellen Conford's lighthearted stories about
young teens' dilemmas started to appear. Frances N.
Chrystie's guide to pet care, *Pets*, first published in 1953,
was revised and reissued in a third edition, and the Favorite Fairy Tales Told Around the World, a series by
Virginia Haviland begun in the sixties, continued to de-
light young readers. Poems by David McCord, one of the
country's best-known poets and first published by Little,
Brown in the fifties, continued to appear in many volumes during the seventies and eighties. In 1976 *Granfa'
Grig Had a Pig*, edited and illustrated by Wallace Tripp,
was named an American Library Association Notable
Children's Book and received the Boston Globe/Horn
Book Award.

Another illustrator whose work appeals as much to adults as to children is Trina Schart Hyman, who has been publishing with Little, Brown since the days of Helen Jones and whose best-known titles include *King Stork, Snow White, The Sleeping Beauty*, and *How Six Found Christmas*. In 1985 Hyman won the Caldecott Medal for her illustration in *Saint George and the Dragon*, retold by Margaret Hodges.

Two interesting and quite dissimilar titles were published in the early 1980s — one looking back at all the riches of children's literature, the other looking ahead to the new themes of social realism and enlarged definition of sexual roles. *The World Treasury of Children's Literature* edited by the well-known writer and editor Clifton Fadiman appeared in 1984, followed by a second volume in 1985. In 1981 *Oh Boy! Babies!* by Alison Cragin Herzig and Jane Lawrence Mali, which told how a group of boys at a private New York school take a course about how to care for infants, won an American Book Award for children's nonfiction.

Thus the age of social realism shows no sign of fading. Children's books now have a strong sense of honesty and deal with life realistically. This direction has been particularly evident in the works of John Langone, aimed at the twelve-year-old and older child, which have contributed much to the understanding of such subjects as mental illness, death, sex, violence, and alcoholism. Another book in the same mode, aimed at a younger age group, is *No More Secrets for Me* (1984), in which Oralee Wachter writes simply and candidly about the increasingly serious problem of sexual abuse of children. The book was an enormous success, and on September 10,

1984, Abigail Van Buren devoted her entire "Dear Abby" column to *No More Secrets*. "This plain-speaking little gem," she wrote, "is written for children of all ages. . . . I do not overstate my enthusiasm when I say that no home with a child between the ages of two and fourteen should be without it."

In the mid-1980s children's books enjoyed a boom as the generation of parents born in the 1950s became determined to share the experience of good books with their children. Libraries, too, ordered in larger quantities than they had in the recent past. Little, Brown, sensing this trend, started to expand its children's program when John Keller returned as publisher in 1985.

More recently, Melanie Kroupa, longtime successful editor of the Atlantic Monthly Press's children's book department, joined Little, Brown as editor in chief of a new imprint, Joy Street Books, bringing all her projects and many authors when the Atlantic Monthly Press decided to stop publishing children's books and focus on adult publishing activities. Their lists burgeoning with talented authors, old and new, the children's book editors at Little, Brown look forward to a bright future.

18

A New Association, 1962–1970

L ittle, Brown marked its one hundred twenty-fifth anniversary in 1962 with the publication of *One Hundred and Twenty-Five Years of Publishing*, a short but attractive history of the company, and by the receipt of many congratulations from authors, friends, and well-wishers. Cornelia Meigs, a long-term author, wrote, "How greatly significant . . . the work of Little, Brown has been. A publishing company, when it fulfills its highest possibilities, can be so very much more than a successful business enterprise or a vehicle for the literary output of its time; it can be, beyond that, an integral part of the civilization of its period."[1]

During the anniversary year the transfer of responsibility from Arthur Thornhill, Sr., to his son took place. Arthur H. Thornhill, Jr., was named president and chief executive officer; J. Randall Williams was made senior vice-president; and George Hall, treasurer, was named a director of the company. The board of directors at this time consisted of these men and Alan Anderson, trade

sales director; Fred Belliveau, general manager of the
Medical Division; Ned Bradford, trade editor in chief;
A. Bradlee Emmons, production director; E. Richmond
Gray, Chicago area manager; James Plate, general man-
ager of the College Division; and Rodney Robertson,
general manager of the Law Division.

The first and most pressing need addressed by Arthur
Thornhill, Jr., was for more space: 34 Beacon Street was
bursting at the seams. Fortunately Little, Brown was
able to purchase a sturdy office building at 41 Mount
Vernon Street, just one block up the hill from the company's headquarters, to accommodate the increase in
staff brought on largely by the growth of the college,
medical, and law departments. This growth also demanded a more sophisticated management structure, so
a finance committee was established and new accounting
systems instituted. Equally pressing was the need for a
larger and more efficient distribution center and warehouse. The ideal piece of land was found, in Waltham,
Massachusetts, and was purchased in January 1963.

The anniversary year also saw the company's entry
into trade paperback publishing. Trade paperbacks are
softcover books of more lasting manufacture that are
sold primarily in bookstores, as compared with mass-
market paperbacks, which are more popular and are sold
in drugstores and supermarkets as well as bookstores.
Mass-market paperback publishing had been important
for the last twenty years, and Little, Brown had owned a
10 percent share in the mass-market house Bantam
Books since the 1940s. Now trade paperbacks were becoming more popular; the company saw an opportunity
and took it.

The Thornhill Building, 41 Mt. Vernon Street

Home of the Medical, Law, and College Divisions — 18 Tremont Street

All this expansion required considerable capital investment. Historically a profitable enterprise, Little, Brown had managed to found its new medical and college text operations as well as expand the existing trade and law programs by retaining profits. To support the kind of aggressive growth that would allow the new divisions to reach their full potential, however, substantial new sums would be needed. Little, Brown was not alone in facing this problem. Wall Street had become interested in the book-publishing business, leading many older firms either to seek expansion capital from the general public or to merge with other companies. Random House, for example, had gone public in 1959. Such moves resulted in more intense competition, which in turn required yet more capital.

In 1965 Thornhill decided to retain outside consultants to analyze the company's fiscal situation and make recommendations for the future. Their report dealt with the alternatives of a public stock offering or the procurement of venture capital and long-term debt. At this point there was no thought of any kind of merger with another firm. Nevertheless, several companies did approach Little, Brown management to suggest a merger, only to be rebuffed. Little, Brown was under no pressure; the balance sheet was strong and management was primarily concerned with long-term strategy.

Then in 1967 Thornhill was approached by Robert Manning of the Atlantic, and a luncheon with his old friend Frank White, a member of Time Inc.'s corporate development staff, was arranged. At the luncheon White suggested the possibility of a merger with Time Inc., and Thornhill, favorably impressed, discussed the matter with the board of directors. They agreed that the proposition warranted further consideration.

Thornhill next met with various Time Inc. executives, including Edgar Baker, director of corporate development; Rhett Austell, publisher of Time-Life Books; and James Linen, the president, who assured him that Time Inc. would guarantee the preservation of the company name, its location in Boston, its present management, and, most important of all, its editorial independence. Thornhill enthusiastically recommended to the board the opening of negotiations, which were authorized, and by the end of the year the terms had been agreed upon. The price was established at 170,000 shares of Time Inc. common stock, and subsequent operational stipulations were outlined and agreed to in an exchange of letters between Linen and Thornhill. Governmental review and approval required considerable time, however, and the merger was not finally completed until August 1968.[2]

The new arrangement turned out to be fruitful for both parties. Time Inc. honored its promises and provided intelligent guidance; Little, Brown continued to grow and prosper, following its directions as established over so many years. One benefit of the merger was that the Time-Life Books series were marketed to retail booksellers through the Little, Brown sales staff. For a number of years large quantities of these handsome, well-illustrated books on specific subjects in art, nature, and history had been sold by direct-mail campaigns to subscribers. Now most of them could also be obtained in bookstores as individual titles. Since then the scope of Time-Life Books has expanded to include cookery, photography, home repair, health, sailing, legends, and many other subjects.

The new arrangement with Time Inc. in no way interfered with Little, Brown's long-standing agreement with the Atlantic Monthly Press, which continued to work as satisfactorily as ever. The two firms remained good business partners, good neighbors, and good friends. In 1964 Director Seymour Lawrence left, eventually to establish his own very successful imprint, and Peter Davison took charge. A skilled editor and poet, Davison had brought to the Atlantic list a host of important poets, including George Seferis, Nobel laureate of 1963. Davison served as director of the press until 1978 and then stayed on as an editor until 1986.

The trade list of the 1960s remained strong. Fiction got off to a good start in 1961 with J. D. Salinger's *Franny and Zooey*, which was the object of more national magazine and newspaper attention than any novel of recent years. At the end of the decade *The French Lieutenant's Woman* by John Fowles achieved critical and popular acclaim and stayed on the best-seller list for many months. *King Rat* by James Clavell launched a notable new author, and a few years later *The French Connection* by Robin Moore did the same. Allan Eckert, C. S. Forester, and Peter De Vries were all steady contributors; the more sophisticated attitude on the part of editors was exemplified in the publication of Gore Vidal's best-selling, controversial novel *Myra Breckinridge*. From the Atlantic came the long-awaited first novel by Katherine Anne Porter, *Ship of Fools*, in 1961, and James Alan McPherson's *Hue and Cry*, the first novel by a young black writer who later won a Pulitzer Prize for *Elbow Room*. Not only did these novels do very well as books, many of them were made into highly successful movies.

Nonfiction was equally impressive. Little, Brown's usual strength in history and biography was displayed by William Manchester's *Arms of Krupp*, Clifford Dowdey's *Virginia Dynasties*, and further volumes in the biographies of Grant, Jefferson, and Washington by Bruce Catton, Dumas Malone, and James Thomas Flexner. Louis Sheaffer's *O'Neill: Son and Playwright* appeared in 1968; the second volume of this noted biography, *O'Neill: Son and Artist*, won a Pulitzer Prize in 1974. News writer and analyst Alexander Kendrick's *Prime Time*, a life of the famous newscaster Edward R. Murrow, appeared in 1969. In 1970 Basil Davidson inaugurated his series of books on the history of Africa with *The African Genius*, an Atlantic–Little, Brown book. *In Defense of Nature* by John Hay was an example of an increasing number of nature books on the list, and Stephen Birmingham's *Right People* was a portrait of the American social establishment.

The famous playwright Lillian Hellman joined the ranks of Little, Brown authors with *An Unfinished Woman* (1969), the first volume of her unconventional autobiography. Soon to follow were *Pentimento* (1973) and *Scoundrel Time* (1976); all three were republished in one volume in 1979 with new commentaries by the author and an introduction by Richard Poirier. From her New Orleans childhood through her adulthood, Hellman hated hypocrisy and refused to settle for soft answers. In her autobiographical volumes she wrote honestly and unsparingly about herself and those around her. She could also be dramatic, funny, and moving, and her tales of New York in the twenties, Hollywood in the thirties,

Arthur H. Thornhill, Jr.

Arthur Thornhill, Jr., and James Linen

Spain during the Civil War, and Russia in the forties and sixties were enthusiastically received by both public and critics.

Little, Brown ended the sixties in excellent shape. The trade operation was solid and growing; the medical list had achieved maturity; the College Division was poised to compete effectively in its chosen area; and the Law Division had recaptured its older strength through increased attention to the student market. The successful merger with Time Inc. had brought the firm financial underpinnings that could lead only to a sounder future.

19

Support and Service Departments

No history of a publishing company would be complete without a description of the many departments whose activities are less conspicuous than those of the directors, managers, and editors, yet are indispensable to the smooth operation of the company's complex business. They include the various copyediting, production, art, promotion, and selling functions and the support services of the departments that handle storing and shipping, management information, accounting, personnel, and corporate maintenance of the physical plant.

In the beginning the firm consisted of the partners, who served also as editors, clerks who kept the records and handled correspondence and accounts, and the movers and handlers of the books. Over the years, the tasks involved in publishing books became much more numerous and specialized. In the late nineteenth century the distinction between the editing of books and their production became sharper. Then the editorial task itself began to subdivide. Editors focused on acquiring an author, then working with him or her to revise and reshape the manuscript to make it the best possible. This type of substantive editing grew even more complex in the divisions other than Trade where a whole host of editors and authors "develops" a book.

At the same time copyediting began to assume more importance. An editor concerned with overall organization, emphasis, wording, and nuance of a book cannot pay much attention to commas, spelling, hyphenation, grammar, even paragraph breaks. This sort of line-by-line, word-by-word attention to a manuscript is quite another skill, requiring a different mind-set. Thus copyeditors became intrinsic to the whole editorial process. Today all the divisions maintain copyediting departments, although the number of copyediting personnel varies from division to division. The Medical and College divisions, for example, almost entirely free-lance the basic copyediting responsibilities, and the in-house copyeditors are much more closely allied with the overall development and production of the books. The Law and Trade divisions, on the other hand, have staffs of in-house copyeditors whose responsibilities not only include monitoring punctuation, grammar, and spelling details but also merge more closely with the larger editorial ones, such that they more properly should be called line editors. A sensitive and careful copyeditor can help an author in many ways. The collateral jobs of proofreading and index making in all divisions, incidentally, are almost without exception free-lanced, since these demanding jobs require time and skills not usually available to the busy in-house staff.

As typography, technology, and book design grew in

sophistication over the years, the production departments became more and more important. Especially in the last twenty years, during which the whole industry has moved from hot-metal typesetting into computerized, photo-offsetting, a great deal of exceedingly specialized technological knowledge has been required. The various production departments at Little, Brown are thus fully staffed with experts. Under their guidance are designers who can translate all the aspects of complicated manuscript material into type and illustration; production coordinators who deal directly with compositors, printers, and binders; paper buyers who keep abreast of the paper needs of forthcoming books and arrange for the right amount to be on hand at the right time and in the right place. Other designers in the art departments create and lay out attractive, eye- and mind-appealing jackets.

Then there is promotion. The adroit placement of an advertisement, the appropriate press release describing a new book, the scheduling of an author's personal appearance all make a tremendous difference in the sales of a book. From what was once merely an announcement in a company-produced catalogue or an ad in a newspaper or the *Bookman* to today's vastly more complex endeavors to bring the books published to the forefront of public attention, promotion and publicity have expanded a thousandfold. The various sales departments essentially have the same goal; an army of salespeople in each division is spread throughout the country, calling on bookstores, colleges and universities, law and medical schools, libraries, and any other location where books might be sold. Today's society requires visibility, and that is what these departments are all about, for if the public does not know about the books, how then will they be able to read them?

If, then, the public becomes interested and wants to get the books, to buy them, they must be available. When a book is ordered — by a bookstore, a library, a college, a marketing middleman, an individual — a whole chain of events is set in motion. Fifteen miles from 34 Beacon Street, in Waltham, is the Fulfillment Center, where books are stored and billed and from which they are shipped.

Before 1909 shipping and warehousing were handled at several different locations. When the firm purchased the Cabot house in that year, an annex at the back of the building was perfectly suited to serve as a warehouse. Shipping and receiving took place on the first floor; the billing office was on the second; trade inventory on the third; and law inventory on the fourth. The operations of the firm were on a scale small enough to fit comfortably into this space until the 1920s, when the increased volume necessitated the construction of a new warehouse adjacent to the bindery in Cambridge and connected to it by a network of bridges and walkways.

Then, at the end of the 1940s, this building proved to be too small, and the need for more space became urgent. Arthur Thornhill, Jr., undertook a survey of the bindery operation and determined that it was no longer economical to operate. Therefore, the machinery was sold and the building converted into an additional warehouse; the bookbinding operations were contracted out. These were, however, merely stopgap measures; as the company continued to grow, it became apparent that a new and larger warehouse would be required.

In 1963 the company purchased the land in Waltham,

just off the circumferential highway Route 128, and a
brand-new warehouse (called the Fulfillment Center)
was built, with sixty-nine thousand square feet of floor
space. Ground breaking took place in July 1963, and by
January 1964 the building was completed. In just a few
days, more than 1½ million books were moved in from
the warehouse and an additional quantity from storage
at various binderies.

Company Treasurer George Hall had investigated
other publishers' warehouses and incorporated into the
Little, Brown building's design all the features he saw as
most useful, so that the new building contained conven-
iences lacking in its predecessors. Moreover, Little,
Brown had had the foresight to purchase adjoining par-
cels of land as they became available to provide for expansion if necessary. So from the beginning the new
warehouse worked well, and when in 1967 the expected
need for more space arose, a thirty-six-thousand-square-
foot addition was quickly constructed. In 1969 the company took over the distribution of Time-Life Books to
bookstores, and the New York Graphic Society became
part of Little, Brown in 1974. These operations required
still more space, such that by 1980 the center had increased by another ninety-four thousand square feet.

The manager of the Fulfillment Center since 1983 has
been Floretta Duane, a vice-president of the company,
under whose expert guidance managers direct traffic
flow, warehouse operations, and customer service, with
a staff able to carry out the tasks efficiently and cost-
effectively. Orders must be processed, invoices prepared,
inventory assessed, royalties calculated, subscriptions
honored, customers satisfied, sales analyzed. Systems for

picking and packing books have become increasingly automated. Recently the firm purchased a Levimatic book-packaging machine, which packages, imprints, and labels single copies, then feeds, loads, closes, seals, and labels the cartons. The machine can pack up to sixty-five cartons a minute, compared with the old manual rate of seventy to one hundred packages an hour.

Customer Service provides the company with a useful point of view from which to gauge reader reaction to publication and services; it is also a public relations branch of the company. Inquiries, compliments, and complaints come in from people everywhere: doctors, lawyers, authors, bookstore clerks, professors, students, agents, even in-house staff. The Customer Service representatives deal with a myriad of requests, from the most routine to the most unusual, such as the call from a woman who wanted a refund for the veal she had ruined when following a recipe in one of the company's cookbooks. Of course, the customer is always right, so the Customer Service representatives must be both diplomatic and effective, and they must also winnow out from the inquiries information that will provide a basis for better service in the future.

An integral part of the Fulfillment Center is the management information system (MIS), which allows the company's general managers and the administrators of the various divisions to monitor budgeting, marketing, administrative, inventory reporting, invoicing, and many other fiscal aspects. Under the direction of William Roberts, the MIS uses a mainframe IBM 4341 system to provide innovative programming and data analysis to the entire company. Programs constantly are refined and new ones developed that are geared to solve special problems. The Fulfillment Center also houses the company's archives.

Treasurer and Vice-President Paul McLaughlin oversees the accounting operations. The Accounting Department, supervised by Controller William R. "Rick" Hall, has five sections. The General Accounting Department takes care of day-to-day bill paying, accounts payable, record keeping, general-ledger entering, expense and income reporting, and payroll administration. Two sections, Credit and Accounts Receivable, work hand in hand: the Credit Department sets credit limits, monitors customer payments, watches over balances due and overdue, and handles collection problems, while Accounts Receivable applies credits to the correct accounts and notifies the Credit Department of any problems.

The Royalty Department is in charge of paying royalties, setting up on the computer the specifics of each contract, overseeing the contract provisions, handling queries from authors about their royalties, and alerting editors to any problems. The Cost and Inventory Department tracks each book, so that all bills for a given title are included and an accurate unit bound cost is determined. This section also handles the physical inventory, making sure that books claimed in the general ledger are actually at the Fulfillment Center. All these accounting sections provide the company with needed information for projecting earnings, budgeting effectively, and making strategic plans for the future.

Another department whose functions extend into every division in the company is Human Resources, overall responsibility for which is in the capable hands of

Fulfillment Center, 200 West Street, Waltham

William Roberts and Floretta Duane

Paul McLaughlin and Judith Kennedy

Vice-President Judith Kennedy. For a long period in its existence Little, Brown, like other publishers, flourished without a formal personnel department. Times, of course, have changed, and the task of ensuring that the best-qualified people are hired so that jobs can be performed creatively and accurately is extremely important. The Human Resources Department, under its director, Cynthia Mathews, receives more than four thousand applications for employment per year and screens and interviews about a thousand of the applicants in the light of knowledge of all available positions. The department also is aware of the special talents of its existing work force so that mutually beneficial transfers within the company can be carried out. Through equal opportunity and affirmative action programs, it encourages and develops a diverse employee group with equal opportunity for all.

The Human Resources Department also administers employee benefit programs and such staff development programs as divisional meetings, in-house training, counseling, and performance and salary review. In connection with the Corporate Services Department, Human Resources issues a bimonthly in-house newsletter that allows employees throughout the company — who are divided among the three Boston buildings and the Fulfillment Center in Waltham — to know about all the goings-on.

Winthrop Hodges, the manager of Corporate Services, who reports to Treasurer Paul McLaughlin, oversees the maintenance, construction, and general well-being of all of Little, Brown's properties. He is responsible for seeing that the oil tanks are filled at the beginning of winter, that the elevators work, that there are enough type-writers, chairs, lamps, and desks. He also oversees the mail and shipping rooms, as well as the all-important files and archives.

All these departments contribute to the smooth operation of a complicated and diverse business. The net result is the continued growth of the company and the enhancement of its reputation as a publisher of quality books — which is what this all comes down to. Today it takes a great many people. No doubt Charles Little and James Brown would be amazed at the number, but we think they would hardly be surprised.

20

Present Tense,
1970 and Beyond

On January 2, 1970, Arthur Thornhill, Sr., died while lunching at his customary table at Locke-Ober, where he had enjoyed so many meals with his associates. It was, perhaps, an appropriate setting for the departure of a man who had enjoyed fifty-seven years of active and successful publishing. His memorial service at King's Chapel in Boston, attended by hundreds of authors, publishers, associates, and friends, was not only an occasion of mourning but also a celebration of a life well lived.

With the memory of that career as inspiration and with the resources of Time Inc. behind him, Arthur Thornhill, Jr., decided to broaden the operations of the company overseas. Little, Brown began to play a more active role at the annual Frankfurt Book Fair and developed closer relationships with foreign publishers, aided in its drive by Time Inc.'s widespread news-gathering network and its holdings in Rowohlt Taschenbuchs in Germany and Editions Robert Laffont in France. Time's Books and Arts Associates handled the liaison among the various firms, and Thornhill worked closely with Zachary Morfogen, director of the Books and Arts Associates, as well as with Ledig Rowohlt and Robert Laffont.

Another Time Inc. connection first bore fruit in the 1970s. This was a series of books from the magazine *Sports Illustrated*, some of them high-level instructional books, such as *Vic Braden's Tennis for the Future* by Vic Braden and Bill Bruns; some more general appraisals of sports and society, like *Super Spectator and the Electric Lilliputians* by William O. Johnson, Jr., a survey of the impact of sports on television and vice versa; and some straightforward biographies or books by sports heroes, such as *Bobby Orr: My Game* by the famous hockey player and *Bear* by University of Alabama football coach Bear Bryant and John Underwood.

It was just as well that the company had these new sources of income, for publishing in the 1970s was going through considerable change, much of which made it more difficult to build a predictably profitable trade list. Firms were growing larger as more consolidations took place. Requirements for public reporting and accountability were stricter. Publishers became more dependent on the services of lawyers, financial experts, and various other specialists; instituted more strategic planning; and developed management systems to control more complex activity and make use of advancing computer technology. The increase in the number of college graduates and the "information explosion" resulted in a great demand for all types of books. Meanwhile, the bookstore chains made books available in hundreds of new locations.

There was, however, a downside to all this activity as far as trade publishing was concerned. The public overwhelmingly elected to buy books by known authors of proven popularity, so that establishing a new author became more difficult, and the bookstore chains, which were interested in quick turnover, were reluctant to stock "middle of the list" books. Thus successful authors could command large advances, and the competition for them intensified. The number of agents increased, partly because the commissions could be substantial, and they modified their offering procedures. Instead of submitting a manuscript or proposal to only one publisher at a time, the agents began to submit material to several simultaneously, a technique known as multiple submission, and there were more auctions of "hot" books during which publishers bid on a rotating basis.

At the same time there were now fewer "professional" writers. Many authors wrote only one book about their own specialties or experiences. Actors, businessmen, athletes, and gardeners entered the field, and publishing became more trendy. For all these reasons the trade acquisition process became much more complicated, and the amount of money invested in future publications increased substantially.

Little, Brown's traditional policy had been to build its own authors, bringing them up through the ranks, so to speak, but now it decided to sign up additional successful authors with well-established reputations. One of these was Norman Mailer, whose first book with Little, Brown, *Of a Fire on the Moon*, grew out of a *Life* assignment about the Apollo moon landing. In 1979 Little, Brown published Mailer's *Executioner's Song*, a novel based on the life and death of Gary Gilmore, a convicted Utah killer who sought his own execution. Considered by many to be the author's finest work, the book won the Pulitzer Prize for fiction in 1980. More controversial was *Ancient Evenings*, published in 1983. Hailed as a masterpiece by some critics, deprecated by others, it was at the very least a considerable literary event.

Another highly successful novelist, whom Little, Brown acquired in what was considered one of the publishing coups of the early seventies, was Herman Wouk. Only after the most careful scrutiny did Wouk select his new publisher. He and Mrs. Wouk visited Boston and spent a full day at 34 Beacon Street, speaking with everyone they met, from the top of the building to the bottom. They were intensely interested in the people who worked for the company, and obviously the staff made a good impression, for Wouk decided that Little, Brown should publish his next book, the immensely successful *Winds of War*, which appeared in 1971.

To celebrate its publication, Wouk decided he would give a party for his publisher rather than the other way around and arranged a jubilant affair at the Copley Plaza Hotel. All who had had anything to do with the book were invited, from company officials and editors to the man who shipped the proofs, the designer of the advertisements, and the writer of the advertising copy, together with their spouses. Mrs. Wouk was there with the Wouks' two sons, who gave warmhearted speeches in appreciation of their father. It was a memorable evening.

The Winds of War was followed in 1978 by the equally successful *War and Remembrance*. The first has already been made into a popular television miniseries, and the second one is following that route. Meanwhile, *Inside, Outside*, a lighthearted yet touching novel based on

Wouk's own youthful experiences, was successfully published in 1985.

The long Little, Brown tradition of publishing first-rate mysteries and thrillers continued during the seventies. Several older practitioners of the art, including Ngaio Marsh and the Atlantic's Geoffrey Household, added titles to the list. A dazzling newcomer, Martha Grimes, appeared in 1981 with *The Man with a Load of Mischief*, the first in a line of books taking their titles from English pub signs. This book and her subsequent ones have put her right among the top-drawer mystery writers.

Humor, another Little, Brown strength, was exemplified by the works of Peter De Vries and the perennially popular Ogden Nash, whose *The Old Dog Barks Backwards* (1972) was unfortunately the last one of his thoroughly delightful creations, for he died in 1971. As other older humorists died or retired, their places were taken by new ones. Among them were the Atlantic's Roy Blount, Jr., whose *About Three Bricks Shy of a Load* was published in 1974, and the cartoonist Berke Breathed. Breathed's sly, satirical Bloom County cartoon strip was syndicated by the *Washington Post* and was appearing in the *Boston Globe* when it caught the enthusiastic attention of Little, Brown's editors. They immediately signed up the young man, and the first book, *Bloom County "Loose Tails"* (1983), sold well over a half-million copies. The subsequent books, *'Toons for Our Times* (1984), *Penguin Dreams* (1985), and *Bloom County Babylon* (1986), have sold and continue to sell in the millions.

On a more serious note, the Dance to the Music of Time series by Anthony Powell — considered to be one

of the most impressive works of fiction of the twentieth
century — continued through the decade, and John
Fowles contributed several outstanding works of fiction,
including *The Ebony Tower*, a collection of short stories,
and the novels *Daniel Martin*, *Mantissa*, and *A Maggot*.
Thomas Pynchon, another fine writer, published a collection of long-out-of-print short stories with Little,
Brown in 1984. A distinguished newcomer joined the list
in 1983 when Ellen Gilchrist's *Annunciation* appeared.
Gilchrist is a notable writer with a distinctive southern
voice whose first collection of short stories, *In the Land of
Dreamy Dreams*, was originally published by the University of Arkansas Press and subsequently republished by
Little, Brown. Her second collection, *Victory Over Japan*
(1984), won an American Book Award, and she is well
on her way to becoming a major literary figure.

Little, Brown's traditional excellence in history and biography was also maintained during these years. Many
distinguished multivolume biographies noted in earlier
chapters were concluded, and the longtime Atlantic–
Little, Brown author Catherine Drinker Bowen wrote
her last popular biography, a life of Benjamin Franklin
entitled *The Most Dangerous Man in America*. William
Manchester made one of the most important contributions to the house through such outstanding books as *The
Glory and the Dream*, a narrative history of the United
States from 1932 to 1972; *American Caesar*, a biography of
General Douglas MacArthur; *Good-bye, Darkness*, a moving account of his experiences in World War II; *The Last
Lion*, the first volume of a biography of Winston Chur-
chill, which became a leading best-seller; and *One Brief
Shining Moment*, a tribute to John F. Kennedy on the
twentieth anniversary of his death.

Particularly notable for their subject matter were C. Vann Woodward's *American Counterpoint: Slavery and Race in the North-South Dialogue* (1971); *Discovery of the Asylum: Social Order and Disorder in the New Republic* (1971) by David Rothman; and the startling and controversial *Time on the Cross: The Economics of American Negro Slavery* by Robert W. Fogel and Stanley L. Engerman, which was published in 1974 and won the Bancroft Prize for history in 1975.

Several distinguished series of collected papers and memoirs were a feature of this period. *The Papers of Adlai E. Stevenson*, edited by Walter Johnson, started with volume I, *Beginnings of Education, 1900–1941*, published in 1972, and concluded in 1979 with volume VIII, *Ambassador to the United Nations, 1961–1965*. George F. Kennan's memoirs were published as an Atlantic–Little, Brown book, and the two volumes of Nikita Khrushchev's memoirs attracted much attention in 1971 and 1974. A successful biography of Henry Kissinger by Marvin and Bernard Kalb appeared in 1974 and was followed at the end of the seventies by the first volume of Kissinger's memoirs. This was a blockbuster project for which Little, Brown competed hotly with at least six other major publishers. A source close to Kissinger said that choosing between publishers in New York and publishers in Boston "was like choosing between ancient Rome, where everything must be done today, and Athens, which produced less of immediate moment and more of enduring value." Arthur Thornhill commented, "Dr. Kissinger and his representatives made it plain from the outset that it was not just a matter of money. He was looking for a publisher who could handle the book with a degree of professionalism and for people with whom he could work compatibly."[1] Evidently Little, Brown's reputation as an outstanding publisher of history played a major part in Kissinger's decision. *White House Years*, published in 1979, and *Years of Upheaval*, in 1982, were widely and favorably reviewed and became worldwide best-sellers.

A commentary on world events from the perspective of an observer rather than a participant came in the two volumes of well-known journalist William L. Shirer's reminiscences: *20th Century Journey: The Start*, which covered the years 1904 to 1930, and *20th Century Journey: The Nightmare Years*, which dealt with the rise of fascism in Germany during the years 1930 to 1940. Donald Spoto wrote two notable biographies, *The Dark Side of Genius*, a life of Alfred Hitchcock, and *The Kindness of Strangers*, whose subject was playwright Tennessee Williams. A valued and productive author of both fiction and nonfiction, Stephen Birmingham, contributed *Certain People* in 1977; *"The Rest of Us"* (1984), a companion piece to *"Our Crowd"* chronicling the story of Eastern European Jews in America; and the best-selling novels *The Auerbach Will* (1983) and *The LeBaron Secret* (1986). Vance Packard, another successful veteran author, added strength to the list through *The People Shapers* (1977) and *Our Endangered Children: Growing Up in a Changing World* (1983).

Little, Brown was by no means limited to history and biography for its nonfiction list. During the 1970s the war in Vietnam preoccupied the United States, and Atlantic–Little, Brown published one of the best-known and most enduring books about that conflict, Frances FitzGerald's *Fire in the Lake* (1972), winner of both the Bancroft Prize in history and the Pulitzer Prize for general nonfiction in 1973. Works on China became popular as that vast nation began to open up. Among the leaders were the Atlantic's *800 Million: The Real China* by Ross Terrill, and Lucien Pye's *China* and Han Suyin's *The Morning Deluge: Mao Tse-tung and the Chinese Revolution.*

Something of the unpredictable nature of trade publishing is illustrated in the fates of two Atlantic–Little, Brown books published in the eighties. *Blue Highways,* William Least Heat Moon's account of his travels across America on back roads and his discovery of his country and himself, was published in 1983 without fanfare, then leaped onto the best-seller list, where it remained for month after month; it is now well on its way to becoming a classic. In the same way, *The Soul of a New Machine* by Tracy Kidder, the story of the race to develop a new computer and of a dynamic modern industry, not only earned a firm place on the best-seller list but won both a National Book Award and a Pulitzer Prize in 1982.

In 1974 Little, Brown embarked on a new kind of trade publishing activity — the tie-in of books with television programs and series. The first project was Jacob Bronowski's *Ascent of Man.* This was followed by a long list of fine books and productions: James Burke's *Connections*; Jack Shepherd's *Adams Chronicles; The Romagnolis' Table* by Margaret and G. Franco Romagnoli; *Life on Earth* by David Attenborough; *This Old House* by Bob Vila and Jane Davison; and *The Aristocrats* by Robert Lacey. Evelyn Waugh's *Brideshead Revisited*, which had been on the list since 1945, took on new life with the airing of the superb British television presentation. Still another outstanding television-associated series was the one made up of the Crockett garden books. Initiated by *Crockett's Victory Garden* by James Underwood Crockett in

1977, the garden books were guided by Boston Senior Editor William D. Phillips over many years. Editor and author took this somewhat prosaic field and made it attractive and glamorous through profuse color photography and artistic design. The first book was produced in record time as a result of good teamwork. It became not only a publishing success but also a model for other publishers preparing books on such subjects as cooking, decorating, and home entertainment.

During the 1970s the Trade Division expanded in yet another direction when it took under its wing the New York Graphic Society, the distinguished graphics and fine-art publishing house. Started in the 1930s by Anton Schutz, this company originally published graphics and fine-art reproductions, later adding books. In 1966, after Schutz's son Herbert had become president, the two men sold the company to Time Inc. Eight years later Rhett Austell, in charge of all Time Inc. book activities, asked Arthur Thornhill, Jr., to take over as chairman of NYGS. Thornhill accepted and moved the book operation from Greenwich, Connecticut, where the print operation remained, to Boston. Such early works as the UNESCO World Art series and *The Complete Letters of Vincent van Gogh* had won for NYGS an immediate reputation for prestigious, high-quality art book publishing, one that continues to this day.

Approximately twenty-five titles appear on the NYGS–Little, Brown list each year, about half of which are new hardcover books developed, edited, and produced in-house, representing a mix of museum publications, imported books, and paperback reprints. There is an active backlist of some two hundred titles, with particular strength in photography, art history, decorative arts, architecture, and American art.

Since 1968, NYGS has been the exclusive trade distributor for publications by the Museum of Modern Art. These include the landmark Picasso retrospective catalogue, the much-acclaimed Works of Atget series, and Beaumont Newhall's classic *History of Photography*, now in its fifth edition. The editing and publishing of exhibition catalogues are among NYGS's specialties; in recent years it has worked with the National Gallery in Washington to produce *The Search for Alexander* and *El Greco of Toledo*, and with the Pennsylvania Academy of the Fine Arts for *Contemporary American Realism*. The tradition of publishing distinguished titles in the field of art history has continued with such books as *Paul Cézanne: The Watercolors, a Catalogue Raisonné*, by John Rewald, which came out in 1984.

In the fall of 1974, the work of Ansel Adams appeared for the first time under the NYGS–Little, Brown imprint, and a long and fruitful association began. A remarkable man, Adams was a true professional who insisted on a superior performance from everyone, including himself; at the same time he was always generous and considerate. A special relationship developed among Adams, his business adviser Bill Turnage, and George Hall and Arthur Thornhill of Little, Brown. New York Graphic Editors Janet Swan Bush and Betty Childs contributed significant editorial expertise and guidance. This association resulted in one of the most successful and longest publishing ventures in Little, Brown's history. Many books appeared, including *Images 1923–1974, The Portfolios of Ansel Adams, Yosemite and the Range of Light*, and a series of technical books on various aspects of photography. Before Ansel Adams died in 1984, he had finished his autobiography; published posthumously in October 1985, it became an instant best-seller. The work of this famous photographer has found a firm and lasting place, and his images will continue to be available in a variety of formats for the enjoyment of future generations.

As photography in general became recognized as a significant art form, the NYGS list included many books by major photographers. The images of Edward Weston, André Kertész, Aaron Siskind, Imogen Cunningham, Henri Cartier-Bresson, Arnold Newman, Joel Meyerowitz, Paul Caponigro, Marie Cosindas, Jerry Uelsmann, Olivia Parker, James Alinder, William Garnett, and Yousuf Karsh were published, as well as books on the history of this genre by James Enyeart, Beaumont Newhall, and John Szarkowski.

Nothing stays the same, in publishing as in any other aspect of human society. The year 1980 saw one of the greatest changes in the history of Little, Brown when the Atlantic Monthly Company was purchased by Mortimer Zuckerman, a successful real estate executive who was interested in publishing. Since 1925 the Atlantic–Little, Brown joint list had enjoyed great success, and many individuals at both houses had worked together amicably and fruitfully. Book publishing, however, changed dramatically in the seventies and early eighties, and it became apparent that the Atlantic Monthly Press itself should assume all the major publishing functions (such as copyediting, production, promotion, and financing) heretofore handled by Little, Brown. At the same time, it

was agreed that it would be mutually advantageous if
Little, Brown continued to provide selling, billing, and
fulfillment services. Therefore a new contract between
the two parties was signed and became effective on January 1, 1985. From that date on, all the new Atlantic
titles were independently produced; only the backlist
books remained under the joint imprint. Various personnel changes also took place during this period. Peter Davison gave up the directorship of the press, remaining as
editor; Upton Brady became the new director. A year
and a half later, in May 1986, Zuckerman decided to sell
the Atlantic Monthly Press to Carl Navarre. The new
owner and Little, Brown worked out a transfer of the Atlantic's children's book program to Little, Brown and
reaffirmed the distribution and selling agreement between the two houses.

There were also changes at the parent company. In
July 1974, Rhett Austell took a leave and Joan Manley,
the publisher of Time-Life Books, assumed his role as
Time Inc. Books Group vice-president. She joined Little,
Brown's board and worked productively with Arthur
Thornhill until her early retirement in 1984[2].

At Little, Brown itself there were changes in the management of the Trade Division. J. Randall Williams,
who had served so ably as the head of the division since
1960, stepped down in 1972, and Joseph T. Consolino,
who had been assistant manager of the division, became
the general manager, a position he handled well until he
left the company in 1979. At this point George Hall,
treasurer and financial head of the firm and a man with
many years of administrative experience at Little,
Brown, stepped in as general Trade Division manager.

He held this position until the end of 1981, when he relinquished responsibility for adult titles to John Maclaurin, who had previously been assistant manager. Hall continued to handle children's books and the NYGS titles for another year, after which they too were passed to Maclaurin, who has maintained the high standards of the trade operation.

For more than fifty years, Little, Brown has kept a New York office to serve the Trade Division. At the present time the office is located at 205 Lexington Avenue. Executive Editor Roger Donald is based there, along with other editors, the entire publicity staff, and senior sales personnel. A presence in New York is important not only in assessing the New York scene but also in maintaining close contact with literary agents, the media, and the subsidiary-rights market.

Although Arthur Thornhill, Jr., has managed the entire company, he has played a special role in the Trade Division, of whose editorial committee he is now chairman. Under Thornhill's management the Little, Brown Trade Division has, despite all the many changes of recent decades, insisted on retaining values that are rooted in the company's history. Quality has always been a fundamental requirement, and though "good books of their kind" may seem a hackneyed phrase, nevertheless it still applies to the publications of Little, Brown, as well as to those of other houses that seem likely to be the most durable.

Changes continued in the eighties as Reginald Brack, Jr., then president of Time-Life Books, was appointed Time Inc. Books Group vice-president to replace Joan Manley, who retired in 1984. He was a veteran of maga-

John Maclaurin

Kevin Dolan, Arthur Thornhill, Jr., and George Hall

zine publishing and had learned continuity book pub-
lishing rapidly as he revived the fortunes of Time-Life
Books. Now he also had to learn about both Little,
Brown and the Book-of-the-Month Club.

During dinner one evening Brack and Thornhill discussed, among other things, the future of Little, Brown
and the subject of succession, since Thornhill was getting closer to retirement and Executive Vice-President
George Hall was approaching his sixties. Thornhill recalled that he had tried to hire Time Inc. veteran Kevin
Dolan to replace George Hall as treasurer when Hall
moved up many years ago. Dolan, however, did not want
to leave New York. Nevertheless, in addition to becoming controller, he had been involved in many book-
related assignments for Time Inc. and recently served on
a book publishing research team. Therefore, an approach was decided upon and happily this time Kevin
Dolan accepted an offer to become president and chief
operating officer of Little, Brown in January 1985.
Thornhill relinquished the presidency but remained
chairman and chief executive officer, and George Hall
was elected vice-chairman. Along with Paul McLaughlin, chief financial officer, and Judith Kennedy,
vice-president, Administration, Thornhill, Dolan, and
Hall make up the general administrative team that
works with the divisional general managers.

As the 1987 sesquicentennial approaches, the people at
Little, Brown confidently look forward to meeting the
challenges of the ever-dynamic publishing scene. They
will take time to celebrate, for they are proud of their ac-
complishments and associations.

Appendix

A History of the Colophons of Little, Brown and Company

Since the founding of Little, Brown and Company in 1837, five different colophons have been used to represent the firm. The first one has a meaning that is still defeatingly obscure, although it may represent the coat of arms of one of the firm's founders. The Latin motto *verbum domini manet in eternum*, which translates as "the word of God remains forever," might be considered more appropriate for a publisher of religious books. While Little, Brown published its share of religious material in the nineteenth century, its reputation, of course, depended upon its law and history books.

The first colophon was not used in all of the company's books. This was also true of the second one. Sheaves of wheat appear on a triangular field along with a scroll on which is inscribed "Books the Best Companions," surmounting a shield with the ornate, calligraphic monogram of the firm. This colophon was used from the final quarter of the nineteenth century until 1911, when a new one was designed and adopted.

T. P. Hapgood, a Boston artist, designed the third colophon, which symbolized the firm until 1938. Within the rectangular shape the firm's monogram is grafted onto a sturdy oak tree — as tradition has it, the Tree of Knowledge. Around the rectangle is the Latin motto *non refert quam multos sed quam bonos habeas*. Liberally translated as "fewer and better books," the motto expresses the policy vigorously espoused by the firm and its then president, Alfred McIntyre.

To celebrate Little, Brown's centennial in 1937 a new colophon was commissioned, designed by Rudolph Ruzicka, one of the leading book illustrators and graphic artists of the day. Ruzicka elected to portray the Beacon Monument, in order to place Little, Brown firmly in the context of Boston's Beacon Hill, with all of its historical and literary associations, where the firm has been comfortably ensconced since 1909.

The monument itself was erected to mark one of Boston's early geographic features. In early colonial days the skyline of Boston was dominated by a three-crested peak known as Trimountain, Trimount, or Tremont. "The high central peak, with an elevation of about one hundred and thirty-eight feet above sea level, which was originally known as Sentry Hill, derived its permanent name from an order of the General Court of 4 March 1634/5 that 'there shalbe forthwith a beacon sett on the sentry hill att Boston, to give notice to the country of any danger.' "[1] Once Boston Harbor was suitably fortified and the defense of the land organized, the beacon was withdrawn, only to be rebuilt in 1768, when the Sons of Liberty thought it necessary to have a means of alerting the citizens should the British, sequestered in Boston, become violent.

After the Revolution, it was decided to erect a monument on the spot where the beacon originally stood. "Charles Bulfinch, with the memory of European monumental columns in mind, proposed replacing it by a commemorative Doric column sixty feet high, including base and pedestal, surmounted by an American eagle standing on a globe."[2] The monument was duly erected, only to be demolished in 1811, when much of Beacon Hill was pulled down to provide fill for the Mill Pond in the North End. In 1898 a replica of the monument was put up on the same site, surrounded by a small park — although that park has given way to a parking lot for State House personnel. Tradition has it that the bronze eagle atop the monument is at exactly the same height as the original Trimountain. It is this linkage of colonial and present-day Boston that Ruzicka captured in his colophon design.

The colophon is a spare, plain outline of the monument crowned by the eagle, facing to the left, and flanked by the initials *L B*; in the background is a stylized representation of the typical Beacon Hill skyline. The dotted border of the oval frame gives the impression of an early nineteenth-century mirror.

The Ruzicka motif still endures in the current Little, Brown colophon, although it has been updated to include a rather more modern feel. The oval shape is slightly flattened, the border is less ornate, and the initials of the firm are bolder and more calligraphic. The row of houses has given way to shrubs and shadows around the monument, and the proud eagle now faces to the right, even as the rejuvenated eagle on Beacon Hill does — looking, perhaps, to the sunrise and the future.

Colophons used since 1837

Chapter Notes

1. "A Copartnership"

1. John Quincy Adams was professor at Harvard from 1806 to 1809.
2. Madeleine B. Stern, *Imprints on History: Book Publishers and American Frontiers* (Bloomington: Indiana University Press, 1956), 29.
3. John Tebbel, *A History of Book Publishing in the United States* (New York: R. R. Bowker, 1972–1981), 1:416.
4. George S. Hillard, *A Memoir of James A. Brown* (Boston: privately printed, 1856), 12.

2. The New Firm Prospers

1. Quoted in J. C. Derby, *Fifty Years Among Authors, Books and Publishers* (New York: W. Carleton, 1884), 675.
2. Quoted in C. Harvey Gardiner, *Prescott and His Publishers* (Carbondale, Ill.: Southern Illinois University Press, 1959), 249.

3. Building the Law Book List

1. Quoted in J. C. Derby, *Fifty Years Among Authors, Books and Publishers,* 674–675.
2. Quotations in this paragraph are from Frederick C. Hicks, *Men and Books Famous in the Law* (Rochester, N.Y.: Lawyers Cooperative Publishing, 1921), 155.
3. William Kent, *Memoirs and Letters of James Kent* (Boston: Little, Brown, 1898), 202.
4. *Law Reporter*, November 1853, 414.

4. Building the History Book List

1. C. Harvey Gardiner, *Prescott and His Publishers*, 248.
2. Ibid., 137.
3. For the details of the publication of *Ferdinand and Isabella*, its reception, and Prescott's relationships with his publishers, see Gardiner, *Prescott and His Publishers*.
4. Sparks's career and reputation as historian are fully described in the *Dictionary of American Biography*.
5. Mark A. DeWolfe Howe, *The Life and Letters of George Bancroft* (New York: Charles Scribner's Sons, 1908), 1:261.
6. For the comments on Bancroft's *History*, see Gerard R. Wolfe, *The House of Appleton* (Metuchen, N.J., and London: The Scarecrow Press, 1981), 250; and Howe, *The Life and Letters of George Bancroft*, 1:105–107.
7. The reviews quoted are from the Little, Brown publicity brochure *Francis Parkman* (1894).

5. Courtesy of the Trade

1. *Bookman*, June 1897, 374.
2. Eugene Exman, *The Brothers Harper* (New York: Harper and Row, 1965), 231.
3. Elihu Scudder, *Henry Houghton* (Boston, 1897), 68.
4. Ellen B. Ballou, *The Building of the House: Houghton Mifflin's Formative Years* (Boston: Houghton Mifflin, 1970), 75.

6. Quotations and Quillets

1. *Proceedings of the Cambridge* (Mass.) *Historical Society*, April 1906, 69.
2. *Bartlett's Familiar Quotations* (4th ed., Boston: Little, Brown, 1863), Preface.
3. Wilbur R. Jacobs, ed., *The Letters of Francis Parkman* (Norman, Okla.: University of Oklahoma Press, 1960), 2:62.
4. Quoted in *Publishers Weekly*, February 17, 1887.

7. Best-Sellers

1. Laura Shapiro, "A Dinner for Six," *Atlantic Monthly* 245 (January 1980): 82.
2. Robert Seager, *Alfred Thayer Mahan: The Man and His Letters* (Annapolis: Naval Institute Press, 1977), 218.

3. Ibid., 204.

4. Ibid., 210.

8. Thomas Niles and His Firm

1. Charles A. Madison, *Irving to Irving: Author-Publisher Relations, 1800-1974* (New York: R. R. Bowker, 1974), 37. See also Martha Saxton, *Louisa May: A Modern Biography of Louisa May Alcott* (Boston: Houghton Mifflin, 1977), and *Notable American Women, 1607-1950,* ed. Edward T. James (Cambridge: Belknap Press of Harvard University Press, 1971), for the story of the writing and publishing of *Little Women.* The reader should note that the book has never gone out of print.

2. Madison, *Irving to Irving,* 38.

3. *American Literary Gazette* 17 (1877): 117.

4. The poem is "Success is counted sweetest," #67 in Thomas Johnson, ed., *The Complete Poems of Emily Dickinson* (Boston: Little, Brown, 1960). See also Richard B. Sewall, *Emily Dickinson* (New York: Farrar, Strauss and Giroux, 1980), 6, 220-221, 581-583.

5. *Publishers Weekly,* June 9, 1894, 859-860.

9. New Ventures, 1900-1925

1, Thornton Burgess, *Now I Remember* (Boston: Little, Brown, 1959), 98-99.

10. The Expansive Twenties

1. Letter, Little, Brown files.

2. *The Book of the Month: Sixty Years of Books in American Life,* ed. Al Silverman (Boston: Little, Brown, 1986), xiii.

3. John Tebbel, *A History of Book Publishing in the United States,* 3:406.

11. Depression and Celebration

1. Annual Report, 1933.

2, *One Hundred Years of Publishing: 1837-1937* (Boston: Little, Brown, 1937), 68.

3. Edward Weeks, "Alfred R. McIntyre," *Saturday Review of Literature,* December 25, 1948.

4. Ibid.

5. Annual Report, 1936.

6. Letters, Little, Brown files.
7. Letter, Little, Brown files.

12.   The War and Its Changes

1. Paul Reynolds, *The Middle Man* (New York: William Morrow, 1972), 129.
2. Edward Weeks, "Alfred R. McIntyre," *Saturday Review of Literature*, December 25, 1948.
3. Quoted in Clarence Petersen, *The Bantam Story* (New York: Bantam Books, 1975), 9.

13.   Postwar Expansion, 1949–1962

1. Millicent Bell, *Marquand: An American Life* (Boston: Atlantic-Little, Brown, 1979), 401–402.
2. Chapters 14, 15, and 16 discuss each of the divisions in detail.
3. Charles A. Madison, *Book Publishing in America* (New York: McGraw-Hill, 1966), 441.
4. *Book Review Digest*, 1937, 61.

16.   The Law Division

1. Clark Byse, "Fifty Years of Legal Education," speech delivered on May 7, 1985.
2. Quotations in this paragraph are from "A Profile of Richard A. Posner," *Re: L, B*, April 1985, 4–5.

17.   Children's Books, 1925 to the Present

1. Mary Mehlman Burns, "There Is Enough for All: Robert Lawson's America," *Horn Book*, 48 (April 1972): 121–122.

18.   A New Association, 1962–1970

1. Letter to Little, Brown, May 30, 1962, Little, Brown files.
2. For the detailed story of the merger, see Curtis Prendergast with Geoffrey Colvin, *The World of Time Inc.: The Intimate History of a Changing Enterprise, Volume Three: 1960–1980* (New York: Atheneum, 1986), 218–220.

20.   Present Tense, 1970–1986

1. *Boston Globe*, January 12, 1977.
2. For more detail about Time-Life Books and the Time Inc.

Books Group, see Curtis Prendergast with Geoffrey Colvin, *The World of Time Inc., Volume Three*, passim.

Appendix: A History of the Colophons of Little, Brown and Company

1. Walter Muir Whitehill, *Boston: A Topographical History* (Cambridge: Harvard University Press, 1959), 7.
2. Ibid., 81.

Bibliography

Ballou, Ellen B. *The Building of the House: Houghton Mifflin's Formative Years.* Boston: Houghton Mifflin, 1970.

Bartlett, John. *Bartlett's Familiar Quotations.* Boston, 1855 et seq.

Bassett, John S. *The Middle Group of American Historians.* New York: Macmillan, 1917.

Bell, Millicent. *Marquand: An American Life.* Boston: Atlantic-Little, Brown, 1979.

Boynton, Henry. *Annals of American Bookselling, 1638–1850.* New York: Wiley, 1932.

Bradford, Gamaliel. *As God Made Them.* Boston: Houghton Mifflin, 1919.

Brooks, Van Wyck. *The Flowering of New England.* New York: E. P. Dutton, 1936.

Buckingham, Joseph T. *Personal Memoirs and Recollections of Editorial Life.* Boston: Ticknor, Reed and Fields, 1852.

Burgess, Thornton. *Now I Remember.* Boston: Little, Brown, 1959.

Burns, Mary Mehlman. "There Is Enough for All: Robert Lawson's America." Parts 1, 2, 3. *Horn Book* 48 (February, April, June 1972): 24–32, 120–128, 295–305.

Charvat, William. *Literary Publishing In America, 1790–1850.* Philadelphia: University of Pennsylvania Press, 1959.

Cheney, Ednah, ed. *Louisa May Alcott: Her Life, Letters and Journals.* Boston: Roberts Brothers, 1889.

218					BIBLIOGRAPHY

Cheney, O. H. *Economic Survey of the Book Industry, 1930–1931*. New York: R. R. Bowker, 1931.

Derby, J. C. *Fifty Years Among Authors, Books, and Publishers*. New York: W. Carleton, 1884.

Donald, David Herbert. *Liberty and Union*. Boston: Little, Brown, 1978.

Eaton, Andrew J. "The American Movement for International Copyright." *Library Quarterly* 15 (April 1945): 95–122.

Ellsworth, W. W. *A Golden Age of Authors*. Boston: Houghton Mifflin, 1919.

Exman, Eugene. *The Brothers Harper*. New York: Harper and Row, 1965.

Fields, James T. *Biographical Notes and Personal Sketches*. Boston: Houghton Mifflin, 1881.

Flint, R.W. "The Boston Book Trade, 1835–1845." Master's thesis, Simmons College Graduate School of Library Science, 1957.

Gardiner, C. Harvey, ed. *The Correspondence of William Hickling Prescott*. Urbana: University of Illinois Press, 1964.

———. *Prescott and His Publishers*. Carbondale, Ill.: Southern Illinois University Press, 1959.

———. *William Hickling Prescott*. Austin: University of Texas Press, 1969.

Gaskill, G. A. "The Boston Book Trade, 1825–1835." Master's thesis, Simmons College Graduate School of Library Science, 1956.

Hackett, Alice Payne. *Fifty Years of Bestsellers, 1895–1945*. New York: R. R. Bowker, 1945.

Hall, Max. *Harvard University Press: A History*. Cambridge: Harvard University Press, 1986.

Hammel, Lisa. "The Quintessential New Englander." *Yankee* 49 (September 1985): 176.

Hart, James. *The Popular Book in America*. New York: Oxford University Press, 1950.

Hicks, Frederick C. *Men and Books Famous in the Law*. Rochester, N.Y.: Lawyers Cooperative Publishing, 1921.

Hillard, George S. *A Memoir of James A. Brown*. Boston: privately printed, 1956.

Howe, Mark A. DeWolfe. *The Life and Letters of George Bancroft.* 2 vols. New York: Charles Scribner's Sons, 1908.

Hoyt, Edwin P. *The Improper Bostonian: Oliver Wendell Holmes.* New York: William Morrow, 1979.

Jacobs, Wilbur R., ed. *The Letters of Francis Parkman.* 2 vols. Norman, Okla.: University of Oklahoma Press, 1960.

James, Edward T., ed. *Notable American Women, 1607–1950.* 3 vols. Cambridge: Belknap Press of Harvard University Press, 1971.

Johnson, Allen, and Dumas Malone, eds. *Dictionary of American Biography.* 20 vols. New York: Charles Scribner's Sons, 1928–1936.

Johnson, Thomas, ed. *The Complete Poems of Emily Dickinson.* Boston: Little, Brown, 1960.

Jones, Helen L. "Early Boston Publishers of Children's Books." Parts 1, 2, 3. *Horn Book* 45 (February, April, June 1969): 20–28, 153–159, 329–336.

Kent, W., ed. *Memoirs and Letters of James Kent.* Boston: Little, Brown, 1898.

Kilgour, Raymond L. *Messrs. Roberts Brothers, Publishers.* Ann Arbor: University of Michigan Press, 1952.

Lord, Melvin. Manuscript of projected history of Boston booksellers. American Antiquarian Society, Worcester, Mass.

Madison, Charles A. *Book Publishing in America.* New York: McGraw-Hill, 1966.

———. *Irving to Irving: Author-Publisher Relations, 1800–1974.* New York: R. R. Bowker, 1974.

Mott, Frank Luther. *Golden Multitudes: The Story of Bestsellers in the United States.* New York: R. R. Bowker, 1947.

Newsome, Florence. "The Predecessors of Ticknor and Fields." Master's thesis, Boston University, 1942.

One Hundred and Twenty-five Years of Publishing: 1837–1962. Boston: Little, Brown, 1962.

One Hundred Years of Publishing: 1837–1937. Boston: Little, Brown, 1937.

Oppenheim, E. Phillips. *The Pool of Memory.* Boston: Little, Brown, 1944.

Paige, L. R. *History of Cambridge, Massachusetts.* Cambridge, 1877.

Petersen, Clarence. *The Bantam Story.* New York: Bantam Books, 1975.

Prendergast, Curtis, with Geoffrey Colvin. *The World of Time Inc.: The Intimate History of a Changing Enterprise, Volume Three: 1960–1980.* New York: Atheneum, 1986.

Proceedings of the Cambridge (Mass.) *Historical Society,* April 1906.

Reynolds, Paul. *The Middle Man.* New York: William Morrow, 1972.

Rheault, Charles. *In Retrospect: The Riverside Press Story.* Privately printed, Boston Society of Printers, 1971.

Saxton, Martha. *Louisa May: A Modern Biography of Louisa May Alcott.* Boston: Houghton Mifflin, 1977.

Scudder, Horace E. *Henry Oscar Houghton.* Cambridge: The Riverside Press, 1897.

Seager, Robert. *Alfred Thayer Mahan: The Man and His Letters.* Annapolis: Naval Institute Press, 1977.

————. *Letters of Admiral Alfred Thayer Mahan.* Annapolis: Naval Institute Press, 1977.

Sewall, Richard B. *Emily Dickinson.* New York: Farrar, Strauss and Giroux, 1980.

Shapiro, Laura. "A Dinner for Six." *Atlantic Monthly* 245 (January 1980): 80–84.

Sheehan, Donald. *This Was Publishing.* Bloomington: Indiana University Press, 1952.

Silver, Rollo G. "The Boston Book Trade, 1800–1825." Parts 1, 2, 3. *Library Quarterly* 15 (October, November, December 1948): 487–498, 557–573, 635–650.

Silverman, Al, ed. *The Book of the Month: Sixty Years of Books in American Life.* Boston: Little Brown, 1986.

Stern, Madeleine B. *Books and Book People in Nineteenth Century America.* New York: R. R. Bowker, 1978.

————. *Imprints on History: Book Publishers and American Frontiers.* Bloomington: Indiana University Press, 1956.

Stone, Orra L. *History of Massachusetts Industries.* Vol. 1. Boston and Chicago: S. J. Clarke Publishing, 1930.

Story, William Wetmore. *The Life and Letters of Judge Story.* Boston: Little, Brown, 1851.

Tanselle, William. *Guide to American Imprints.* Cambridge: Belknap Press of Harvard University Press, 1972.

Tebbel, John. *A History of Book Publishing in the United States.* 4 vols. New York: R. R. Bowker, 1972–1981.

Tryon, W. S. *Parnassus Corner: A Life of James T. Fields, Publisher to the Victorians.* Boston: Houghton Mifflin, 1963.

Weeks, Edward. "Alfred R. McIntyre." *Saturday Review of Literature* (December 25, 1948): 20–22.

Weston, George F., Jr. *Boston Ways.* Boston: Beacon Press, 1957.

Weybright, Victor. *The Making of a Publisher.* New York: Reynal, 1966–1967.

Whitehill, Walter Muir. *Boston: A Topographical History.* Cambridge: Harvard University Press, 1959

Winsor, Justin, ed. *The Memorial History of Boston.* 4 vols. Boston: Ticknor and Co., 1880–1881.

Wolfe, Gerard R. *The House of Appleton.* Metuchen, N.J., and London: The Scarecrow Press, 1981.

Illustration Credits

James Kent, painted by Asher B. Durand; reproduced courtesy of
The Harvard Law Art Collection

William Prescott, painted by Joseph Alexander Ames; reproduced
courtesy of the Massachusetts Historical Society

Jared Sparks, painted by Rembrandt Peale; reproduced courtesy of
The Harvard University Portrait Collection, Bequest of Lizzie
Sparks Pickering

George Bancroft, painted by Gustav Richter; reproduced courtesy
of The Harvard University Portrait Collection, Bequest of
George Bancroft, 1891

Thomas Niles; reproduced courtesy of Yale University Library and
Farrar, Straus and Giroux

Alfred R. McIntyre: photograph by Dorothy Wilding

Edward Weeks: photograph by Dorothy Wilding

Samuel Eliot Morison: photograph © Karsh, Ottawa

Arthur H. Thornhill, Sr.: photograph by Fabian Bachrach

Niels Buessem; Chester C. Lucido; Timothy C. Robinson; Melanie
Kroupa and John Keller; The Thornhill Building; 18 Tremont
Street; Fulfillment Center; William Roberts and Floretta
Duane; Paul McLaughlin and Judith Kennedy; John Mac-
laurin; Kevin Dolan, Arthur Thornhill, Jr., and George Hall:
photographs by Alan Oransky

Arthur H. Thornhill, Jr.: photograph © by Jill Krementz

Index